Now That's What I Call Jargon

John Murray

**NEW
ISLAND**

Now That's What I Call Jargon
First published 2008
by New Island
2 Brookside
Dundrum Road
Dublin 14

www.newisland.ie

Copyright © John Murray, 2008

The author has asserted his moral rights.

ISBN 978-1-84840-019-1

British Library Cataloguing Data. A CIP catalogue record for this book is
available from the British Library.

Typeset by TypeIT, Dublin
Printed in the UK by Cox & Wyman

10 9 8 7 6 5 4 3 2 1

For my parents,
Vivian and Nancy

Contents

Introduction

In 2003, I became a business journalist with RTÉ. My career up to then had been a mixture of politics, broadcasting and general newspaper reporting, so the idea of getting into a speciality raised eyebrows among friends and family who had never quite seen me as someone who would take to scouring balance sheets for a living. My banker brother even sent me a couple of books on the basics of business and economics to help me cope with the challenges that lay ahead.

Another former colleague suggested that I go for a day course with an accountant to get some instruction on how to read balance sheets. But, in a grand display of risk-taking, I gave the training suggestion a miss and began my life as a business broadcaster. With the help of my new colleagues, I managed to pick up lots of information along the way and by the second month I was churning out figures for pre-tax profits and underlying earnings per share as if I had been weaned on them. I was talking about 'EBITDA – Earnings Before Interest, Tax Depreciation and Amortisation' – like a seasoned stockbroker and, if some of the figures contained in those preliminary results before me were a little bit confusing at seven o'clock in the morning, I consoled myself that radio listeners could take in only so much information in the one go. If they were really interested in the minute detail of the balance sheet, they could read the results themselves online or pick up the business pages of the newspapers the following day.

So, after a while, I found that I could deal with the figures, but what I had not bargained for was the need to learn a 'foreign' language to get by in business journalism. I had some vague notion beforehand that business terms would take a bit of getting used to, but I was not prepared for the sheer volume of jargon that was about to head in my direction. At that stage, email was already in full flow and every public relations firm was happy to send it to the RTÉ Business Desk, regardless of its newsworthiness. I had been in the job only two days when a representative of one public relations firm offered me a 'heads up'. Maybe I had lived a sheltered life until then, but it was the first time I had heard the expression. Three years on, an average week brings with it at least a dozen 'heads up's. It is not illegal; it is just PR-speak for giving notice of an event.

This was just the beginning of an education that would soon lead me to discover that 'suites' were not just nice hotel rooms or furniture for the sitting-room and that 'boutiques' were not just places where designer clothes were sold.

Three years on, far from the fog lifting, it has got thicker. A survey carried out by a British recruitment company, Office Angels, has revealed among office workers a growing intolerance of the use of terms such as 'blue sky thinking', 'singing from the same hymn sheet', 'thinking outside the box', and 'park that thought'. In 2007, a public company in the UK, Sports Café, which operates a chain of themed bars, ran into trouble for issuing a profit warning that no brokers could understand. The statement from the company said that its board was meeting to 'establish the quantum of this trading deviation'.

But do not be fooled into thinking that this peculiar way with words is evident only overseas. Across the length and breadth of Ireland, business people are driving business performance across a multitude of platforms in order to achieve a paradigm shift. Or they are using their core competencies to create additionality in a fast-moving environment.

Some are developing their multi-functional capabilities in order to move up the value chain, going forward, while others are happy to concentrate on the key deliverables that will enhance their value proposition. Others merely believe that business is all about the bottom line, and stepping up to the plate – after kicking the tyres, of course. Where once there were plain links, there are now connectivity, synergies and partnerships. Employers wake up in the morning with the onerous responsibility on their shoulders of up-skilling their workforce in order to better embrace the knowledge economy.

Politicians may be the leaders in the field, but business people are rapidly becoming adept at providing answers that do not easily fall into the 'yes' and 'no' categories. In addition, the statements that many companies prepare now are crafted so cautiously that it often takes half a dozen readings to establish the real meaning, if, indeed, there is one.

Companies also have difficulty trying to announce bad news in a straightforward way. For instance, a whole string of words has been invented to deal with that most common of experiences for businesses – reducing the number of people they employ. It used to be a case of laying off workers, but now the exercise is as likely to be described as 'right-sizing' or 'de-hiring'.

The old-fashioned concept of 'calling a spade a spade' seems to have disappeared. And if there was a world league for 'jargon penetration', Ireland would be vying for one of the medal positions. We use jargon and clichés with abandon. Blame whom you like, but the period of our remarkable economic growth over the last 15 years has brought with it a strange new version of the

English language which has become part of everyday communication. You should not have to travel too far to find it. It is spoken in boardrooms, in conference halls and on our national and local airwaves. It is written in our newspapers, business manuals, and consultancy reports.

We are 'rolling-out' and 'driving' and 'tasking' and 'ramping up' with enthusiasm. There is a strong American influence, including those overused baseball terms that at least have simplicity to recommend them. But let's not apportion all the blame to the 'suits' across the Atlantic. Surely Wall Street cannot be blamed for the rapid spread of that ugly term 'going forward'? Perhaps corporate America is a little more culpable for 'to do' becoming 'to action', and for customers suddenly becoming 'revenue-generating units'. Yet nobody put a gun to our heads and insisted that we speak or write like this. So why do we use this new language with such enthusiasm?

One explanation could well be that, in the same way that our new-found wealth has many of us looking no further than the latest car model in the garage forecourt, so too we have become convinced that we have to speak jargon-laden English if we are to be fully paid-up members of the global economic club.

Then there is that element of self-importance, the author or speaker more interested in impressing his or her peers than in sending a simple message to the readership or audience. There is undoubtedly a view among some business people that the more specialist terms they use, the more people will be convinced of their high intelligence.

But it is not merely a matter of the business people of Ireland feeling good about themselves. Public companies will go to great lengths to dress up mediocre news when they issue trading statements and financial results. Simple English in these written productions is as rare as an Irish heatwave. Some of the statements often disguise the real news that is contained within them. The authors clearly hope that analysts and stockbrokers, no lovers of plain English, will miss the point and provide a better than expected verdict on the company's fortunes – and keep shareholders happy in the process.

Jargon is also evident at another level. Small companies vying for business in a small market like Ireland believe their chances of winning customers will be enhanced if they present their skills and talents in a language one or two notches above normal human discourse. The business that some of them do drum up only goes to prove the theory that you *can* fool some of the people some of the time.

But the abuses are not just confined to business. In the health service, there is regular talk of 'patient flows' and 'step down' beds and 'outcomes'. Politics has created a new breed who work 'around issues', 'embrace change', and 'implement strategic reviews'.

Sometimes the use of jargon can be a result of muddled thinking, gobbledygook messages being transmitted from brain to mouth and uttered unthinkingly. It is also very convenient for those public figures who are not on top of their subject to hide behind jargon, in the knowledge that the people around them are unlikely to question it, for fear of being exposed themselves.

So what? I can already hear some people saying. The English language is constantly evolving and why shouldn't there be new ways of saying things? Why be prissy about it? Surely all that matters is that the message is communicated clearly and, beyond that, there should be no argument. Does it really matter whether it's the Queen's English or some less elegant twenty-first-century form? This is not a matter of life and death, and is not worthy of serious debate, I hear the sceptics mutter.

Well, apart from simple taste, there is a serious side to this. Just ask the National Adult Literacy Agency. It estimates that 70 per cent of people find it difficult to understand basic application forms for financial services. It has discovered that even people with high literacy skills are left scratching their heads a lot of the time.

The Financial Regulator, whose job it is to keep an eye on banks, building societies and insurance companies, has a team of people whose task it is to translate the language of the banking world into understandable English.

As you will discover in this book, recruitment ads are also written in the sort of language which would leave potential job applicants wondering if it is a job in retail they are reading about, or a role in the mission to discover life on Mars. Is it acceptable that State agencies, funded by the taxpayer, should publish reports containing passages that are at best complex and at worst unreadable? Ireland, a country that prides itself on its literary past and its social and communication skills, has become a safe haven for jargon.

Perhaps we shouldn't be surprised. Ireland, after all, is home to some of the world's biggest IT companies, and they are unbeatable when it comes to infecting the English language with verbs, nouns, adjectives, and hyphenated horrors that did not exist ten or fifteen years ago. We should give them full credit for the delights of connectivity, downtime and offline. We should offer them our thanks for giving us time-line, interface and bolt-ons.

Perhaps they never envisaged that their own particular dialect would become so much a part of general discourse. But when you are presented with a copy of a booklet entitled *Preferred Terms for the ICT Community*, unprompted, you do wonder if the 'techies' believe that IT-speak will soon be the only means of communication.

Jargon is also very evident in public life. Politicians often speak in a language that is not too easily understood beyond the confines of Kildare Street. Trade union officials, and indeed journalists, also have their moments, as you will discover.

I decided to write this book following the success of a feature on jargon on the weekly RTÉ Radio One programme *The Business*. It has become apparent from the reaction of listeners to the programme that not only are the jargon samples a source of great mirth, but they have also sparked off a good deal of debate about how our language has reached such a sorry pass.

Without getting too carried away with it, many listeners have appealed to us to continue our campaign to try to stave off the contamination of the English language. They regularly send us examples, some of which are featured here.

This book is intended to be both informative and entertaining. I do not profess to have exclusive rights to, or a monopoly on, plain English, and am often guilty of using some of the words and phrases that would easily qualify in any modern-day definition of jargon. I scold myself regularly for asking interviewees for the 'time-frame' of a certain proposal when 'how long will it take?' would make much more sense, and am also conscious that I promise to 'touch base' with people more than any other daily activity. A listener recently criticised my use of the term 'soft landing' and I also did my own bit of verb creation when I asked a colleague to 'business card' me someone's mobile phone number.

Perhaps it is the sign of a mundane life, but there is nothing quite as enjoyable for me nowadays as hearing a jargon-free interview or reading a jargon-free press statement. In fact, listening to good communicators is such a breath of fresh air, in sharp contrast to the human polluters who can be heard frequently on the airwaves, or whose repugnant prose is being fed to newsdesks every day via press statements.

If this book discourages the use of hackneyed expressions, sees the disappearance of some tired jargon, and encourages a more straightforward approach to the language, it will have performed some service. At the very least, I hope it puts a smile on your face and raises the odd chuckle or two about the lengths to which some people will go to say a lot without really saying anything.

Here's to plain English.

Chapter 1
Going Forward

Freedom of speech is an important right in any democracy, but should there not be an equal responsibility to speak with some degree of meaning? These are the weighty matters that pre-occupy us on the RTÉ Business Desk. Well, me anyway. As I embark on interview after interview on the morning business news or on the main *Morning Ireland* programme, I ask myself is it good enough to let every onslaught on the English language go unpunished? To misquote former Taoiseach Jack Lynch once more: 'Should we stand idly by?'

Take business interviews. If I am confused about what my

interviewee is saying, how do listeners cope without the benefit of a press release in front of them and some briefing material? Among the listeners, no doubt, there are business people who can use these terms with ease, but the majority, I guess, are not hearing a language with which they are familiar.

In my dafter moments, I have thought of all sorts of ways to bring a stop to it. One of my early ideas was to halt an interviewee in full flight every time he or she uttered a word such as 'scaleable' or 'portfolio' and ask them to come up with a more easily understood alternative. I realised soon enough that this was not practical, although I might have made it into the Guinness Book of Records as the presenter of the longest business bulletin ever heard on a national radio station.

My second daft idea was to sound a hooter every time a bit of jargon was uttered. My bosses made it clear they did not want the business news sounding like Heuston Railway Station every morning. Bruce Hill, a public affairs radio presenter in Australia, was a bit braver:

> When I do interviews with people in the Pacific and outside the region whom I suspect might try to use this kind of debased public language, I tell them before I start recording the interview that jargon isn't really suitable, and if they start using those sort of words, I will go 'bzzz!', tell them what they did wrong, and ask them the question again. So far I've only had to do that once, and the person I was interviewing took it in good spirit, and admitted that jargon is being used too much these days.

I ended up settling for the less drastic option of pointing the finger or 'naming and shaming', if you will forgive me the cliché, once the offending interviewees had left the building. When I began presenting RTÉ Radio's new weekly programme *The Business* in 2004, I realised that there was plenty of scope for a weekly item on jargon and clichés.

I scoured press releases and job advertisements for examples and, after a while, listeners began to submit their own. In truth, the search for offending words and phrases was never that exhausting, and 'scoured' is probably overstating it. Jargon and clichés are to be found in plenty of places.

A ten-minute trawl through incoming emails to the RTÉ Business Desk was enough. One sample search in October 2006 threw up some typical examples: Fine Gael TD Bernard Durkan criticised government policy for gas and electricity price increases 'at a time when international energy price indicators are on a downward trajectory'; Tim Cowhig from the Irish Wind Energy Association informed us that 'wind makes up a significant part of our energy portfolio going forward; the Progressive Democrat TD Tim O'Malley told us that the problems of Moyross had been 'well-ventilated'; Waterford's County Manager alerted us to the presence of a 'suite of incentives'; The Minister for Enterprise, Trade and Employment, Micheál Martin, explained what we had to do to achieve a 'knowledge-based, innovation-driven, participative and inclusive economy'. At the same event, the chief executive of CPL Resources, Anne Heraty, stated that 'Ireland had an opportunity to drive economic development through building skills capability'.

These are not just any speakers, but people in positions of influence in politics, business and the public service. And they can be assured that unless the language becomes simpler, they too will get the treatment on *The Business*.

In a nice compliment to the programme, one or two chief

executives told me that their main concern during interviews was not so much the prospect of tough questions they might be unable to answer but replies that might subsequently feature in the jargon item on *The Business*. So much for my tough questions.

One of our strongest campaigns has been to eliminate the term 'going forward' from common use. We do not know exactly where it began its life, but it has suddenly taken up a position at the end of thousands of sentences. It is more often spoken than written. Politicians and business people are the main offenders, and seem to use it because normal words escape them.

This willingness to 'go forward' is a positive expression, undoubtedly, but when it finds its way into so many sentences uttered by people in high places, it does become tiresome. During one interview in 2005, the then Minister for Finance and now Taoiseach, Brian Cowen, used the term 'going forward' on eight occasions during a seven-minute interview. We pointed this out in *The Business* the following weekend and when he continued to use the term in a subsequent interview, we gave him a pointed reminder again.

Thankfully, Cowen's use of 'going forward' has become less common recently. He even managed to introduce three Budgets without using the phrase. But his cabinet colleagues do not seem to have got the message. In 2006, the then Minister for Transport, Martin Cullen, decided that 'going forward' of itself was not enough. He suggested that the recently privatised national airline, Aer Lingus, should be 'going forward into the future'! Such faith in the passage of time was touching.

Aer Lingus chief executive, Dermot Mannion, is another man fond of 'going forward'. I recently lost five euro wagering a colleague that he would use the term 'going forward' four times during a radio interview. He used it five times. Still, we have made progress. One of Mannion's other favourite expressions is 'value proposition'. In a recent interview, he had replaced it with the more easily understood 'business case'. The objections to 'going forward' have nothing to do with the phrase's complexity; it is just one of those terms that adds nothing to a sentence.

'At the end of the day' is in the same category – and yet begins many sentences. What difference is there between 'At the end of the day, we must make sure that everyone in our society feels valued' and 'We must make sure that everyone in our society feels valued'? 'At the end of the day' can occasionally be given a breather and replaced by 'at this moment in time' or 'in the final analysis' and they all share the distinction of adding little or nothing to our fund of knowledge on a particular subject. In the same family falls 'the reality is', and again, just listen next time to an interview on radio or television and count just how many times it is used. It has become unbearable through overuse. Just think how funny it would be to state the opposite: 'The reality isn't ...' See? It makes no sense at all.

If these meaningless phrases have any redeeming quality, it is that they do not confuse or complicate. The same cannot be said for the language used by some agencies in receipt of public funding. Take for instance the J.E. Cairnes Graduate School of Business & Public Policy at NUI Galway. To get some idea of what goes on there, you don't even have to set foot on campus. Just read the college's Research Directory and learn about some of the Graduate School's initiatives:

> COBERA is a loose group of academic researchers based in Ireland, Italy, Denmark, UK, Malaysia, India, the US, Mexico, Brazil and Sweden who are attempting to refashion, retool and replace the neo-classical core

of economic theory with alternative methodological, epistemological and formal concepts more in tune with the zeitgeist in the broadest sense of this word.

At least you know where some of your hard-earned taxes are going! There is a new definition of the three 'r's here – refashion, retool and replace – and discussion of the 'neo-classical core of economic theory' can only be a positive for Irish society.

The Institute of Public Administration is a training body for the public service. The IPA's annual conference theme in 2006, 'Moving Towards the Public Sector of the Future', was unlikely to win any awards for originality, but at least we knew what they were getting at. We became less certain when we began to read the promotional brochure. We were introduced to concepts such as 'new localism', 'citizen engagement', 'stakeholder democracy', and one speaker, B. Guy Peters, Maurice Falk Professor of Government at the University of Pittsburgh, crossed the Atlantic Ocean especially to tell us that 'there is continuing pressure to move away from conventional hierarchical, command and control instruments for government towards the instruments of new governance.'

Perhaps every senior public servant who attended the conference understood perfectly the concepts that were flying all around them, but what about the vagueness and the unnecessary adjectives – is there such a thing as a stakeholder-less democracy, for instance?

And why do conferences bring out the worst kind of English? The Dundalk Chamber of Commerce thought it a good idea to host an event in June 2006 with the theme 'Stoking the Marine Tourism Engine'. If that was not enough to pack the delegates into the Holy Trinity Heritage Centre in

Carlingford, Co. Louth, the targets set for the day were sure to do the job:

> The real and palpable target outcomes of this conference are to focus on key strengths and opportunities that align with established best practice, to encourage the future 'road map' to evolve, along with all stakeholders, public and private, to identify ownership and responsibility to each for their deliverables, and to establish a tracking monitor alongside the creation of this package, ensuring its action points are pursued.

I read this at least a dozen times on first receiving it and even doing so slowly left me with no idea whatsoever what the organisers of the conference were trying to achieve. Having a 'road map' for a marine conference was always going to be a difficult 'sell' for the organisers. Once again it illustrates the ability of some organisations to use language that is seriously bloated and unlikely to be widely understood. Perhaps the work of those who populate graduate schools and public training bodies was never meant for the ears and eyes of a mass audience. But some stab at simplicity would be welcome. That said, they are in good company, as anyone applying for a job today fully appreciates.

Chapter 2
Hiring

There was a time back in the 1980s when Ireland was on the brink of bankruptcy and thousands of our citizens were forced to go abroad in search of employment. That level of emigration is a distant memory now and, as our economy continues to grow, albeit at a slower rate in recent years, Ireland is often held up by organisations like the Organisation for Economic Co-operation and Development (OECD) as a living, breathing example of how small, geographically isolated countries can provide most people of working age with decent livelihoods and a good quality of life.

Ireland still remains very much a place to be, and the growing number of flights, and even bus routes, between here and Eastern Europe is evidence of our growing attractiveness to thousands of people from the new EU states who can come to Ireland and earn multiples of what they would earn at home. The world of work is changing. The 'job for life' is an old-fashioned concept. In fact, some recent research said that most people joining the workforce now could expect to be in five or six jobs by the time they retire. There is more part-time work, less permanent and pensionable employment, and the sort of short-time contracts that place an emphasis on achievement.

The Irish workforce has passed the two-million mark for the first time, and opportunities still abound in many sectors, apart from the job losses in some traditional manufacturing industries that have been unable to withstand the competition provided by lower-wage economies in Eastern Europe Asia, and parts of central America, as well as the recent slump in the construction industry.

'So what has all this got to do with jargon?' you legitimately ask. Well, with more jobs than there are workers to fill them, recruiters have had to become very creative in the means they use to find the brightest and the best. The days when it was sufficient to slap a 'Vacancies: Staff Wanted' sign on the door have come and gone. The emphasis is suddenly on making every job sound as if the successful candidate will soon be rubbing shoulders with Bill Gates and Sir Anthony O'Reilly on the world business stage. The jargon-laden recruitment advertisement is now the norm rather than the exception. Employers seem happy to use the services of those with an astounding ability to write copy that makes even the most menial task sound as if it requires the intelligence of an Albert Einstein.

Some of the creative work comes from the hiring companies themselves, but much of the blame lies with that new breed known as 'recruitment' or 'executive search firms'.

It is evident in many sectors. Take Bank of Scotland Ireland, for instance, a company with a significant presence in the Irish banking market. A business bank until 1999, it then began offering mortgages to personal customers and, with its way of doing business, shook up some of the longer-established institutions. Then in 2004 it went a step further and announced that it was setting up dozens of new bank branches around the country. So, if you are suitably impressed, how do you get to become part of the Bank of Scotland Ireland success story? Well, first you are faced with the not insignificant challenge of trying to understand the bank's recruitment advertisements. Take this one for instance:

An individual is sought with three to five years' relevant experience to lead major projects within core areas of the business which will encompass cross-functional responsibilities and provide extensive exposure to Executive Committee members in a highly commercial, entrepreneurial and driven environment.

The minimum requirement will be a 2:1 degree, a straight-talking creative style, with an ability to deliver outstanding performance and a desire to be very, very successful. The quality threshold is high and the rewards include the opportunity to develop an excellent career in a highly challenging environment.

The bank is clearly trying to attract the thousands of people who leave school every year and tell their career guidance teachers on their way out that their ambition in life is to 'lead major projects within core areas' of a business. For them, this advertisement represented one of those 'eureka' moments.

When they read on and discover that the job also encompasses 'cross-functional responsibilities', they will be doing victory laps around the local housing estate. Perhaps they will not have considered that 'extensive exposure to Executive Committee members' was going to be part of the deal, but, heck, when they find out that this is all going to happen in a 'highly commercial, entrepreneurial and driven environment', they will be reassured.

They will probably have a little chuckle when they learn that a 'straight-talking creative style' is needed. But, blessed with an inner confidence that their forefathers would have been proud of, they will realise that this was just a bit of in-house sarcasm.

For applicants, the most endearing part of the ad, though, is its insistence that they possess a 'desire to be very, very successful'. Not successful, you hear, but very, very successful. If you are in any doubt about what Bank of Scotland Ireland expects from you, its declaration that the 'quality threshold is high' is sure to provide you with the answer you need. And because the rewards include 'the opportunity to develop an excellent career in a highly challenging environment', you won't need to be paid, will you?

In a perfect world, the Bank of Scotland Ireland recruitment ad would be an isolated case – a rare mistaken text that slips through the hands of the proofreaders.

Alas, the creative efforts of a company called Genesis quickly arrives onto the recruitment pages of *The Irish Times* to shatter our illusions. The company takes the following approach to the recruitment of new members:

> Do you look at the world differently? Genesis is a specialist business consultancy focused on developing and implementing customer-centricity as a value-driver for enterprise. This includes designing and managing the project plan, guiding and creating the content of meetings and deliverables and developing client-specific solutions.
>
> We value a can-do orientation, thought leadership and an unrelenting ability to challenge the way things are done.

A quick run through the ad appears to have the desired effect – we do end up looking at the world differently, and wondering if there is no limit to the ability of some to bamboozle others. Genesis considers itself a specialist consultancy 'focused on developing and implementing customer-centricity as a value-driver for enterprise'. To be honest, we have no reason to doubt that it does, for, in truth, we really have no way of knowing, since this is not an English language with which we are familiar.

Sadly, no further clues are provided in the third sentence, and we are just left to ponder how one would create the content of 'meetings and deliverables' and develop 'client-specific solutions'.

As to the values of Genesis, who knows? Its search for a candidate with a 'can-do orientation, thought leadership and an unrelenting ability to challenge the way things are done' is, well, to be welcomed, isn't it? Buried in this advertisement somewhere is a job that someone, somewhere could do, and the money is probably good too. But by the time you have got to the bottom of what the words mean, you may well have reached retirement age.

The challenge for the coffee shop chain Starbucks is slightly different. Its recruitment campaign aims to make the job of serving and waiting on coffee-drinkers sound altogether more fundamental to the future of mankind. Hence, when the company decided to open new shops in Dublin, it came up with the following recruitment ad:

> We like to think of every cup of coffee as having its own distinct personality, full of the flavours and aromas unique to its origins. That same individuality applies to our managers too. It's your strength of character that will make the first-ever Starbucks store in Ireland the finest customer experience yet, whether it's lively conversation with regulars or letting people relax and enjoy their coffee in quiet reflection, you believe that investing time with people is priceless.
>
> That goes for your team as well. After at least two

years managing people in a hospitality or retail environment, you'll know how to inspire them to create the best coffee in the right atmosphere.

Your obvious good conversation and sense of humour should be complemented by a sincere commitment to Dublin's community.

If the tears are not streaming down your face and into your frappuccino at the end of reading this ad, you are a cold-hearted monster. Now, the queues forming at the new Starbucks coffee shops in Dublin may well point to the success of the recruitment campaign and many patrons may be leaving, nodding quietly to themselves and saying: 'Drinking that mocha and eating that muffin represented the finest customer experience I've had in my life'.

The most intriguing part of the ad is its insistence that the candidate show a 'sincere commitment to Dublin's community'. Is an oath of sorts required?

The bold claim that every cup of coffee has its own personality is another eye-catcher. We are pretty sure that Starbucks in Ireland has yet to have a customer approach the counter with his or her regular americano and claim that it is too temperamental, not sincere enough, or not interested enough in them as a person.

The Starbucks ad campaign is clearly an American import, striving to sound folksy and authentic at the same time, and obviously contriving to make jobs that do not have non-stop satisfaction written all over them sound a little more appealing.

Closer to home, the love affair with the hyphen as a central part of the recruiting process continues. The drink and food snack company C&C floated on the Irish stock exchange in early

2005. Its performance during that year surpassed all expectations and one of the starring roles was played by its cider business in Clonmel, Co. Tipperary.

That successful operation was looking for a human resources director, and so it was that the company advertised for one in 2005. The advertisement first pointed out that the vacancy had arisen because of the 'progression of the current incumbent into a new role ...' but what exactly did the cider company require from candidates? Well ... 'your impressive background and career of achievements gained from a fast-moving multi-site environment will be complemented by broad experience in the definition and implementation of HR strategy and policy, as well as designing and driving organisational and cultural change which ultimately brought added value to the bottom line.'

Is it just I who am thrilled with the prospect of working in a 'fast-moving multi-site environment'? If you haven't been in one already, you had better get experience of one quickly or you have not got a hope of getting to the interview stage. And even if you manage to accumulate experience in such an environment, you will then have to look at yourself in the mirror and say with honesty whether or not in your career up to now you have been 'designing and driving organisational and cultural change which ultimately brought added value to the bottom line'.

My hunch is that you will not be too sure if you have or not, but that you may press on and apply and just say a prayer that the question isn't posed at the interview. Not much point staying awake at night asking yourself the question whether you have or not brought 'added value to equal the bottom line'. Thousands of careers have perished over that particular obsession.

As the national broadcaster, RTÉ is keen to promote the idea of itself as a centre of culture and creativity. Slogans along every corridor encourage staff to be creative and, occasionally, the authors of job advertisements in the organisation take things too literally.

The role of Continuous Improvement Manager is one of those job titles that did not exist 20 years ago. For the role RTÉ advertised in 2005, the main responsibilities were 'adopting a recognised model of continuous improvement and learning'. In addition, the successful candidate would be 'assisting and advising on methodologies and their application to continuous improvement projects and other related work'. But that was not all. Responsibilities also included 'training and supporting managers in the understanding and operation of the continuous improvement model adopted, and adopting and implementing a process of tracking and recording continuous improvement to ensure objectives are met and added value is realised and recognised'.

Within hours of this particular vacancy being posted on RTÉ notice boards, a consensus had emerged that the nature of the job was utterly beyond the comprehension of most normal people. Indeed, in some quarters, there was a view that it was beyond the comprehension of even the unhinged. A person was appointed, but not before the offending ad had been taken out and shot at point-blank range in a leafy part of RTÉ's ample grounds.

Mind you, making things unnecessarily complicated is not the sole preserve of our national broadcaster. The retail company Musgraves, which has its headquarters in Cork, began a search for a Food Safety and Quality Manager in 2005. The advertisement that appeared in national newspapers told us that 'the successful candidate will be a pragmatic, solution-driven senior manager comfortable operating in a cross-functional environment'. We had to quickly remind ourselves that Musgraves was in the supermarket business and had not been given the task of looking for a talented new crew for Starship Enterprise. Perhaps we live a sheltered life, and the world is filled with 'solution-driven' senior managers seeking to work in a 'cross-functional environment' – it is just that it sounds so daunting.

A British company, Dixie Henderson, applies a much simpler formula. In search of a Head of Group Communications, Dixie Henderson wanted the successful candidate 'to manage the messages and processes that optimise internal motivation and illuminate external perceptions'. While some job advertisements have nothing whatsoever to recommend them, the idea of spending the day optimising and illuminating sounded like a bit of fun at least.

An Post, the Irish postal service, is a far more complex operation today than in days gone by when it was just a matter of sorting mail bags, sending parcels and letters, and selling stamps. In this era of new technology, it sought a suitable candidate for the post of Engineering Systems and Process Manager. The person specification was as follows:

> With an ability to focus on the big picture, and key deliverables of a project while mastering the important detail, they will be able to anticipate obstacles and provide timely interventions and solutions to ensure successful project delivery.

We have read this a few times and have never been quite able to shake off the impression that the creative hand behind it was a person who did not get out enough.

The need to focus on the 'big picture' is now so ingrained in the recruitment process that it may be sufficient for companies to place in small print at the end of the advertisement a line saying: 'This is a big picture appointment'.

The same applies to that other quality required of the average job applicant nowadays – a 'can-do' attitude. Some companies, of course, hide anonymously behind the recruitment agency. In this instance, the recruiter was Sigmar. The jobs ... well, read on:

> A HR director is required for a large financial services organisation based in Dublin North. This is a fantastic opportunity ensuring that HR initiatives across the organisation are supporting the business strategy. This position involves liaising with business leaders to devise appropriate talent and organisational intervention strategies, working alongside HR generalists to develop resolution strategies, providing training and directing leaders and their respective teams to enhance overall success.
>
> This position also includes shaping the organisation culture through vision and communication and handling complex and executive level employee relations issues.

And what about this one?

> A HR consultant is required for a leading Financial Services organisation. This is a twelve-month contract. It is a relationship management position focusing on delivering HR activities to the business, providing high-quality deliverables, supporting a broad range of recruitment requirements, participate in projects, drive initiatives to improve people capability and manage change programmes.

The grammar in this ad is enough to upset the most relaxed English scholar, but we are pretty sure that there are people around the country who fulfil the criteria set down in these demanding recruitment advertisements.

And just when you think that job ads have a monopoly on complexity, along come some interesting job titles and appointment notices.

One returning emigrant moved from a job in the Decision Science Practice of a company's London office to a role in the Cork office where she would specialise in 'using a benefits management approach to increase the return on change initiatives, in the strategic assessment of telecoms acquisitions'.

We have no reason to believe that the job brought her anything but the highest level of job satisfaction, but another woman who wrote to us on *The Business* did not even get to the stage where she could consider crossing the threshold. The position was with Elan, the Irish pharmaceutical company, and our correspondent was told that the job would suit her since it was 'geography non-specific'. She wondered if this meant she would not have her own desk, but we do know her interest in the job did not extend to her asking exactly what they were on about.

The fun doesn't stop there in the recruitment industry. How couldn't one but be overwhelmed by this 'strategic vision' from executive search firm Propeo International as it tries to entice Irish companies into its web:

> To be a leader in the field of Executive Search services, bringing quality, high-impact solutions to a highly select client base comprised of progressive high-velocity companies, with whom we have strong and dynamic relationships!

Our mission is to partner with our clients in the task of finding and getting on board the best executive talent available to devise and execute their business plans. We are lean, dynamic and motivated, and we focus on delivering exceptional service to our clients, with whom we find a good cultural fit.

Propeo International also tells us it invests in 'leadership capital', but we took that for granted, didn't we?

Or take this, the boast of one our top executive search firms, Merc: 'Our expertise lies in the recruitment of middle and senior executive managers across the complete functional spectrum.'

Another Irish recruitment company, Parc, professes to be 'a leading supplier of tailored recruitment process outsourcing solutions'. It is good to know these things.

In the space of a decade, the recruitment business has been transformed. The days of 'Coffee Shop Opening: Staff Wanted' would have done the trick for Starbucks a decade ago, but it appears that the demands of today are far greater. Could it be that companies competing for staff in an economy enjoying almost full employment feel the need to exaggerate?

Are applicants genuinely taken in by the bold statements, and do some of them end up as happy employees working with personality-filled coffees and fast-moving cider-makers and customer-centric IT consultants? Or is it all being done, without our knowledge, to add to the gaiety of the nation? There are no rules governing recruitment ads and what they contain, apart from obvious matters of public taste and gender equality. The newspapers that have earned so much from recruitment advertising in the years of the Celtic Tiger economy are hardly likely to turn around and tell the recruiters they shall not carry their advertising unless they use plain English and do not make exaggerated claims about the nature of the jobs they are advertising.

As it is, a lot of recruitment has moved from newspapers to the Internet, where verbal excess does not quite fit the medium. There, the rule appears to be that if it cannot be said in one page, it is not worth saying. Perhaps the world would be a duller place if we didn't have that search continuing for people with 'multi-channel capabilities' and 'thought leadership' skills. Sometimes, though, as you browse through those recruitment pages, you say to yourself that the successful candidate will be someone who has read this rubbish carefully, sees it as the work of a HR director with notions, and manages to convince his or her new bosses at the interview stage that stacking the supermarket shelves is within his or her 'skills set'.

I think we have built a strong case against the recruitment industry for atrocities committed against the English language. We may not have proven premeditation in all cases but there appear to be grounds for 'word-slaughter' at the very least. The exciting business of recruiting people obviously sends creative pulses racing and, by the end of the process, is responsible for many ordinary workers becoming 'can-do, self-starting, big picture' candidates. It would be wrong, though, to blame our executive search firms – the posh name for recruitment companies – for all the linguistic sins that are being committed around us.

And it is not all bad: far from it. Every year, awards are given out in Ireland for recruiters who do manage to achieve a combination of creativity and simplicity. What fans of plain speaking yearn for is a return to the days of a slower-moving, big-picture-free environment. It would be just the job.

Chapter 3
Firing

At the best of times, we do not like passing on bad news. We are quicker than Olympic sprinters when there is good news to impart, but when it comes to telling someone that they no longer have a job, or have lost all the money that they invested in that hedge fund, or that they have been outbid on that house of their dreams, we prefer to delegate or to dress it up as not the devastating news that it appears to be at first sight.

In today's image-conscious world, companies have difficulty

being straightforward about bad news. We presume that they are too busy to spend hours with their human resource and public relations people thinking up new ways of presenting the news in a better light, but some time is spent trying to make the unpalatable sound not as painful as it actually is.

It is not that they cannot bring themselves to tell people that they are losing their jobs. That is the easy part. No, in the interests of preserving corporate reputations, they have to find different ways of explaining to the public what they are doing without making themselves sound like ruthless capitalists. It has given rise to a new vocabulary, and created a world where taking a pickaxe and chainsaw to a company's workforce can almost appear like an act of chivalry.

The first rule of expert practitioners trying to 'manage' bad news is almost to deny that anything of a negative nature is happening at all. In this world, there is no room for words such as 'bad', 'difficult' and 'problem'.

For those trying to interpret what is going on – mainly shareholders, stockbrokers and journalists – there is some decoding to be done. Thankfully, overuse has brought with it a certain familiarity, and the warning bells begin to go off when adjectives such as 'challenging' and 'robust' crop up.

In the old days, the term 'losing one's job' was used to describe the experience of someone being in employment one day and out on his or her ear the next. But this is deemed to be very negative talk indeed by today's standards. Nowadays, a company is least likely to say: 'Our costs are too high, we are making less profit and therefore we have no choice but to reduce our workforce and lay off a hundred people.'

The author of such a statement would most likely find themselves the 101st person to be laid off. The 'plain English' approach to bad news is not very evident anywhere. Today, when a company decides that it has too many workers on its payroll, it rolls out the 'r' word – 'rationalisation'. Those workers who are no longer going to be working in the company may not think the idea too rational, but do they really matter?

The media like simple concepts, so a word like rationalisation is heaven-sent in this era of the 30-second news story. Journalists will happily develop it into a 'rationalisation plan'. If they are pushed to explain why it is happening, they will reach for the 'g' word – 'globalisation'.

A good example of the way things are moving was evident in an initiative the Bank of Ireland took in 2004. The bank's newly appointed chief executive, Brian Goggin, decided that the Bank of Ireland was unlikely to keep on making record profits year after year (although it has managed to make a good fist of it in the intervening period). So, he set about some cost-cutting and announced that the bank was going to seek to reduce its number of workers by two thousand, a ten per cent reduction. But what was this laying-off to be called? It just was not fitting for a bank that had made in excess of €1 billion in 2004 to announce a 'voluntary redundancy programme' now, was it? That sounded so 'eighties'. After a fit of boardroom brainstorming no doubt, the bank's plan to shed 2,000 staff was launched as a 'Strategic Transformation Programme'. It was a breathtaking concept and clearly captured the imagination of clerks and tellers in branches up and down the country. By mid-2005, almost 2,000 people had signed up for it.

There was a sequel. In June 2006, the Bank of Ireland announced the latest stage in its Strategic Transformation Programme. A UK support services company, Alfred McAlpine, was given a seven-year contract to provide facilities management to the bank. The contract, the statement said, would ensure that the 'outsourcing arrangement optimises operational costs and services'. Thirty million euro would be saved in the process and more damage to the English language was thrown in as an unexpected bonus.

The sheer brazenness of the Bank of Ireland's approach was in contrast to that adopted by one of the world's biggest computer-makers, Hewlett-Packard, which employs 4,000 people in Ireland. In 2004, the company announced that it would have to reduce costs and, as a consequence, that would lead to job losses. Or would it? After reading this particular statement from the company, you were not too sure:

> Following the recent announcement by Hewlett-Packard that 5,900 jobs within EMEA (Europe Middle East and Africa) would be impacted by workforce management activities, HP confirms today that 204 positions will be impacted in Ireland over the next two fiscal years.

Note the absence of the phrase 'job losses' here – hardly an oversight and perhaps, who knows, the words themselves may be blocked from Hewlett-Packard computers. A new phrase is coined in the first few lines – we had never heard about jobs being lost because of 'workforce management activities' but we are always open to new ideas. And the confirmation that '204 positions will be impacted' raises the odd doubt or two.

Enlightenment was just around the corner:

> However, HP expects that the real impact on its Irish operations will be minimal as a result of redeployment

and hiring into new business areas. HP is the largest IT and Services company in the Irish market and its businesses are performing strongly and are growing. As a result, HP is continuing to hire skilled employees, including engineers and other professionals. HP will also look to re-train or re-deploy existing employees to ensure continued growth of its business in Ireland.

HP believes that these factors, combined with natural attrition, will help to reduce the effect of the restructuring plan and are likely to lead to an overall increase in employee numbers in Ireland over the period.

Now, maybe I have missed something, but has Hewlett-Packard just patented a new invention in the world of business – the job loss announcement that ends with the distinct prospect of extra recruitment? In summary, Hewlett-Packard appears to be saying that it is continuing to hire people in Ireland and to re-train and re-deploy others and reckons that, if you throw in a bit of attrition, the company could end up with an increase in employee numbers over the period.

EMC announced its own bit of cost-cutting in 2005 but the multinational company with a plant in Ovens in County Cork almost had us convinced that this should actually be marked for the attention of the 'good news department'. It went thus:

'EMC has approved a plan to rebalance its workforce, which will result in increased focus on new product development and the company's ability to target, reach and support more customers around the globe.

During 2006 approximately 1,000 positions will be affected as the company expands its sales coverage around the world and grows its product development team. The adjustments are expected to be complete by the end of 2006 and will result in a fourth-quarter 2005 cash charge of approximately $80 million to cover the cost of employee separation benefits.

I don't know about you, but it appears to me that EMC is trying to send a message here that whatever it is the company is doing, it is good for us all. The confusion arises because it throws out that widely used verb 'rebalance'. But the $80 million that the company says is being set aside to pay for employee separation benefits is a giveaway. The separation is between the company and its workers. It will eventually be by mutual agreement, we presume, but we take it that the workers did not go to their employers first and suggest that they be laid off.

By way of clarification, Joe Tucci, EMC chairman, president and chief executive, adds:

> The best companies preserve their leadership by looking out to the horizon and making adjustments today to position themselves for shifts in customers' expectations and market dynamics. Our business model and organisational structure continue to evolve as we integrate new acquisitions, expand into new markets and address more of our customers' needs. While we continue to focus on improving our overall cost efficiencies, we also plan to utilise this rebalancing to invest in sales and R&D in order to accelerate our innovation engine to capture an even greater share of our expanding market opportunity.

When pharmaceutical company Schering Plough announced in 2005 that it would be reducing its workforce by 120, it said it would establish an 'outplacement assistance programme' for those being made redundant. Suddenly, those who were losing their jobs were merely being 'outplaced' and the company was being good enough to provide them with some 'assistance' as well. The company was trying to tell its workers that it cared, minutes after it had told them it did not care quite enough to keep them in employment.

And what about Accenture, a British company that employs in excess of 5,000 people in Ireland? It had decided in 2005 to close its operation in Dublin, with a loss of 150 jobs, but getting the company to say as much proved a little more difficult. The RTÉ Business Desk received a seemingly self-explanatory email from a worker which said that his company, the aforementioned Accenture, would be closing its Dublin services centre which employed 150 people. Bad news, indeed, but simply put. My colleagues immediately followed it up and were given the following statement by the company:

> Exel and Accenture have worked together for nearly 10 years and we continue to support them as a client around the world. Following the acquisition of Exel by Deutsche Post World Net, the company [DHL] has carried out a review of its global operations in this area. As a result, DHL has decided that some of the services currently delivered at Park West in Dublin will be migrated back to local DHL country operations over time.
>
> Throughout this period, we will be working closely with affected staff to understand any opportunities for them in the wider business.

Still not altogether sure still of the status of the Dublin employees, my colleague made further enquiries and got this response:

> We provide service to DHL from Ireland to its other European businesses. Over the next nine to 12 months we will be transitioning some of those services back to their countries on a phased basis. We will then work to redeploy those staff back inside the wider Accenture group.

This was a little clearer, but was it enough for those who were losing their jobs in Dublin? We did not think so. Let us be thankful for the fact that at least no one in Accenture used the 's' word – separation.

This is one of these words that used to be heard mainly in the family law courts, but some senior manager in human resources decided that it was badly needed to freshen up the jaded old language of job losses.

The world's biggest maker of computers, Dell, decided in 2006 to reduce the number of people working for it. Perhaps being an employee of Dell is like being part of a family but, for better or worse, the company unashamedly branded it a 'separation programme'. Someone in *The Irish Times* obviously spotted this phrase and took inspiration from it because they billed their plans to lay off 43 people in 2006 as a 'voluntary parting agreement'.

In June 2006, Oracle Corporation, the American multinational company, issued a statement about its 'restructuring' plans in Ireland. It was evident from its words that getting to the point quickly was not one of its priorities:

Within Ireland, Oracle has enjoyed good growth over the last few years as customers select our product and services to achieve their business goals and be successful. To place us in the best shape to take advantage of future growth opportunities, we appraise our organisation structure on an ongoing basis. Oracle Corporation is currently undertaking a global business re-alignment within the Finance area. Part of this re-alignment will involve a reduction in job roles in Oracle's Shared Service centre, located at both the Dublin and Galway offices. This reduction is expected to be achieved mainly through a combination of re-deployment, natural attrition, non-renewal of temporary short contracts and redundancies, and we will work with employees to assist with the transition. This realignment process will happen over the next 6 months or so. Taking into account the hiring in of new talent, the transitioning employees from our various acquisitions, and the redeployment and redundancy processes, this should result in an overall change in staffing levels in Ireland over the year of a reduction of approximately 2 per cent.

The cries of anguish and frustration that this press release triggered could be heard across Dublin and neighbouring counties on the June evening it was published. In a move of sheer genius, we decided to ring the public relations company representing Oracle and ask them how many people they employed. We would then take out our calculators and do the complex mathematical calculation – workforce minus two per cent equals x.

The company was not very forthcoming. It said it would not give us the details of how many people it employed and repeated the mantra about cuts being achieved through 'redeployment, natural attrition' and 'non-renewal of ... contracts' and left us to ponder the number of people who would become former Oracle employees as a result.

But perhaps Oracle has spent a lot of time studying the modus operandi of its Californian neighbours, Sun Microsystems. On 31 May 2006, the company issued a statement headlined: 'Sun Microsystems Approves Growth Plan to Accelerate Return to Profitability and Sets Operating Income Growth Goals'. The company explains that as a result of 'ongoing analysis', it is 'instituting a number of initiatives to better align expenses with its core business strategy'. Its plan provides for 'increasing investment in core technology and channel resources while accelerating acquisition synergies and disinvestments in non-core processes and research and development activities'.

As people with vast experience of reading these statements, we sense that clarity may be not too far off and, in the fourth paragraph, we find out a bit more about what Sun Microsystems is trying to say as the firm has a brief flirtation with the English language.

> More specifically, the plan addresses several cost-cutting initiatives, including a 11–13% reduction in force and the consolidation of its real estate portfolio. The company is reducing the worldwide employee headcount by 4,000 to 5,000 people over the next six months and is selling its Newark campus and existing leased facilities in Sunnyvale, California.

Yes, buried beneath the waffle and blows delivered to the English language was a paragraph that said almost everything. But 'reduction in force' and 'headcount' are terms that are not included to inject humanity into the process of laying off thousands of your staff.

And therein lies the difficulty, or, in corporate speak, the 'challenge'. George Orwell wrote that 'the great enemy of clear language is insincerity'. When companies say 'growth' when their aim is to 'reduce', they are distorting the truth in order to preserve their reputations. Perhaps it will do no damage to their profitability in the long run, but it should raise public concerns about their true intentions.

All the while, the nature of what exactly is being done remains partially hidden. It would be far preferable for everyone if a company announced that it was reducing by 'x' amount the number of workers it employs in order to save money and so retain its profitability. The limp-wristed and phoney language that makes its way into many corporate announcements smacks of cowardice and deception.

But, in fairness to the Americans, they have put a fair degree of creative effort into finding a more palatable way to deal with bad news. Workers can now be 'de-hired', or even better, be part of a 're-sizing'. There is 'down-sizing', 'rebalancing', 'right-sizing', 'downscaling', and there are 'parting agreements'.

Waterford Wedgwood's former chief executive, Peter Cameron, was happy to tell journalists in June 2006 at the presentation of the company's annual results that the company's 'right-sizing' had been a success. In the previous 12 months, the company had reduced its workforce by 1,800, and closed its manufacturing plant in Dungarvan, Co. Waterford. Forget about the economic arguments. The dispute here centres on the use of proper English to describe a cost-cutting process.

Wyeth, the pharmaceutical company with a big presence in Ireland, had to tell its global workforce in early 2008 that a drug from which it had been making handsome profits would soon have a competitor, and this would have consequences. The company wrapped up those possible consequences in a process it called Project Impact.

The company explained what Project Impact was:

> This is a company-wide program that is designed to take a strategic look at transforming our business in addition to providing new term benefits. The early stages of the project are designed to provide short-term benefits associated with cost reductions and changing workflows and we expect this to benefit 2008. This will include headcount and other reductions, and we expect many of these reductions to take place in the next month.
>
> Longer term, Impact is designed to be a comprehensive program to fundamentally change how we conduct business across the entire company and to adapt to the continuously changing environment. Over the course of the next several quarters, we will refine and validate the longer term opportunities, and we'll provide you more information as the year progresses.

Buried beneath the convoluted language somewhere is a message that the company will reduce the number of people it employs.

Many of the companies that steer clear of the precise truth when the news is bad are equally likely to exaggerate their good fortune when more positive news is on the agenda. Somewhere in between these two states, there are a few simple words trying to get out that might better express the reliance of big business on honest human endeavour to be successful. So when people have to go, the company should just say so, and look after them as best they can as they take their skills elsewhere. They should not insult their employees' intelligence with language that is used to soften the blow but often serves only to infuriate.

Chapter 4
IT Doesn't Make Sense

A recent interviewee on *The Business* was asked to put forward an excuse for his colleagues in the world of Information Technology. 'Why all the unintelligible gobbledygook emanating from your industry?', we asked him.

He argued that some of his colleagues were misunderstood. How could one describe the virtual, the intangible, he asked us, if one could not use some technical terms? They had a far more difficult job than car salesmen, who could quite clearly point out to customers the features that made the sleek machine in front of them worth that extra €5,000. He insisted that they were doing their best to make a good fist of trying to explain something that was complex.

Being polite souls, we looked on him kindly and smiled, and did not tell him what we really thought. What IT consultants say within the four walls of their 'centres of excellence' is undoubtedly a matter for them, but it is when they decide to share it with the wider world that the problems arise. Many people in the IT industry make the complicated sound even more so and achieve a level of acrobatics with the English language that perhaps could qualify as an Olympic discipline.

Announcements of new jobs may be quite common these days, but the human capacity to talk them up as if they were giant steps for mankind remains undiminished. When they are IT jobs, the 'blue sky' is the limit. In July 2005, a statement from the world's biggest maker of computer chips, Intel, was able to tell us that the company was 'to grow its R&D capability in Shannon with 80 new jobs'.

The then Minister for Enterprise, Trade and Employment, Micheál Martin, set the mood by saying that our prosperity depended on establishing a 'culture of scientific and technological innovation'. He told us that the expansion was about the 'world-class track record of R&D execution in Intel Communications Europe (ICE)' and the 'highly developed marketing competencies'.

The thing about gung-ho ministerial statements is that they tend to act as an encouragement to others. No sooner had the minister sat down than Jim O'Hara, general manager of Intel Ireland, was on his feet describing the 80 new jobs as a 'significant milestone in growing our overall mandate here in Ireland'. Already, there is enough 'growing' in evidence to merit a stand at the Chelsea Flower Show. O'Hara also said the expansion would 'enhance our future value proposition for Intel Corporation' and who are we to doubt him? But Jim was not the only Intel kid in town that day.

Up stood Doug Davis, vice-president and general manager of the company's Communications Infrastructure Group, to serve up a menu of 'converged communications processors, modular building blocks, and platform-based solutions'.

Not to be outdone, the then Shannon Development Chief Executive Officer, Kevin Thompstone, chipped in with 'high-value, knowledge-based jobs', 'technology-based investment on a global scale' and 'year-on-year growth plans'. He described it as a 'great win for Shannon' – but who exactly they were playing against, and in what sport, remained a mystery. The local Intel man rounded off the jargon-fest by telling the assembled masses that the local 'pipeline of talent' will help 'grow the operation into the future'.

What did the English language do to deserve such torture?

Moving in the same information technology corridors is the US multinational Cisco Networks, whose Chief Executive Officer, John Chambers, was able to tell shareholders at the publication of another set of positive quarterly results:

> Customers are realising the benefits of an intelligent network architecture and the company is seeing long-term momentum across product families, geographies and market segments.

There was also some wonderful IT-speak in a press release issued in 2005 by EMC. It was announcing a deal between EMC and another American company called Axciom. EMC's Jeff Nick said that the two companies would provide customers with the industry's 'most complete, grid-based information infrastructure for information-intensive applications'. And Charles Morgan from Axciom was equally chuffed:

> By combining EMC's proven track record of innovation and market reach with our established business intelligence leadership, we will be able to deliver a configurable, scalable platform in a single location where services and data content can be manipulated, stored and made available to information-centric applications.

And we have no doubt, Charles, that you will be able to

deliver those 'configurable, scalable platforms' – what with your proven track record of innovation.

But we should not heap all the blame at the door of the multinational companies. Home-grown IT jargon is alive and well. Let us strike out for the south-west of Ireland first and try to grasp the role in life of an IT company based in the Kerry Technology Park in Tralee.

The county has produced some great writers over the years; the names of John B. Keane and Brendan Kennelly come to mind immediately. But on 29 November 2005, evidence of a new writing talent emerged with the news that promotional agency Shannon Development was to provide funding for a company, Freeflow, based at the Kerry Technology Park. It, in turn, would be able to take on 18 new staff members as a result.

So far so good, with the Minister for Enterprise, Trade and Employment, Micheál Martin, describing Freeflow as the type of 'knowledge-based indigenous company Ireland needs to position itself as a leader in the global technology marketplace of the future'. Yes, indeed.

Things become a little bit trickier when it comes to working out what Freeflow actually does. This was the company description:

> Founded in 2001, Freeflow (formerly known as Web Component Trading Ltd) is a provider of a comprehensive suite of inventory asset management solutions that leverage the power of the Internet and combine it with business services to manage slow-moving or obsolete inventories. Freeflow's offering helps customers maximise asset recovery and profitability, increase inventory cycle turns while avoiding channel

conflict, and reduce overall reverse logistics costs . . .

Freeflow is headed up by a team of industry veterans that collectively bring more than 75 years' domain expertise in the manufacturing, logistics, financial and supply chain arena. The company has recently undergone a re-branding which now allows it to move and develop into other verticals seamlessly.

'Leverage' is one of the star verbs of the twenty-first century. There isn't a business in the western world that does not leverage something or other. 'Solutions' is one of the star nouns of this present century. Any IT company worth its salt offers some class of solutions or another.

If we move up along the west coast to Galway, we encounter another company whose use of words is exemplary – if you love jargon:

The focus in the coming 12 months will be on seeking to maximise efficiencies to be gained in its multi-channel capabilities by addressing the process flows of a variety of business operations.

So said a statement from Graham Technologies issued on behalf of Fiona Graham, managing director of this company. The sentence represents the polar opposite of that childhood cry: 'We know what you're doing'.

Please read that sentence fifteen times, and if you discover what Graham Technologies is actually doing, kindly write to us and let us know. 'Maximising efficiencies' is one of those ugly phrases that are sprinkled liberally throughout the world of Irish business. We think it means doing business the best way possible.

Its use is slightly – just slightly now – more excusable than the awful combination that is 'multi-channel capabilities'. We think it means being able to do loads of different things, perhaps at the same time, but we are still at the head-scratching stage.

There are probably people who set out in life with the aim of addressing process flows but, if so, we have yet to meet them.

Perhaps they were being helpful when they subsequently sent us on details of a new product. The press release, the company spokesman said, contained details of an 'exciting new product agent 247' which is 'a process-centric intelligent agent for self-service, which allows users to interact with computer systems in a more human-like manner'.

Wireless Networks Ireland is based in Dublin and we know what it does do – don't we? The company is Ireland's leading provider of wireless networking solutions, focusing on the hospitality sector. Founded in 2003, the company says it 'leverages the strength of its partnerships to bring best-of-breed wireless solutions to customers, backed by a comprehensive range of professional services'. It goes on: 'What makes Wireless Networks Ireland unique from any other company of its kind in Ireland is that we offer our customers a fully managed end-to-end solution for their wireless requirements.'

This is classic jargon. It contains 'leverages' and 'solutions' in the first sentence, no less. And the writer had a good dose of the horrid hyphens – with his 'best-of-breed wireless solutions'. And just in case you were in any doubt about the type of solutions the company provides, we discover in the final lines that they are 'end-to-end' ones. This prose may be easy to understand, but it doesn't take away from its ugliness.

And what about PlanView Enterprise? Its website tells us it

... combines total business demand management with real-time portfolio analytics, best-of-breed resource management and action-driven processes. Working together, these elements give customers total IT visibility, fewer redundancies, increased efficiency and the ability to focus limited resources on higher value work. By integrating analytics with root-cause analysis, PlanView Enterprise enables true optimization, yielding even greater efficiency and productivity.

A browse of the Internet unearthed the following linguistic flourish, courtesy of the website www.idc.com: An Industry Focus: Using ICT to Improve Business Processes and Develop Innovative Business Strategies.

For MCI, business innovation must have an equal focus on service as technology per se. This is particularly important in today's convergent business environment – service providers must work flexibly to support customers evolving business needs, no matter how complex the challenge. It's about providing the right portfolio of solutions, but also meeting the operational and strategic goals of today and tomorrow. Technology providers must therefore become true business partners, with an in-depth understanding of customers' business drivers, an encyclopedic technological know-how, and the intelligence to think beyond the 'now' to ensure that solutions are future-proof.

So is it perfectly acceptable that companies in the IT industry speak their own language, and leave us ordinary mortals grasping for any sense of meaning from the sidelines? Should we lose sleep over it? Do we need to find some 'end-to-end ... best-of-breed solutions' for our own lives? Maybe, and then again maybe not, but perhaps the IT professionals should wait until we leave the room, or, like the social pariah smokers, go outside and do their own 'leveraging' in the back garden.

Chapter 5
In Bad Company

We are not quite sure at what stage in the climb up the career ladder that chief executive officers start speaking in a different language, but we do know that seniority brings with it a certain tendency to begin 'embracing' a new language. It is almost as if they started their careers in business with good, old-fashioned plain-speaking in mind but quickly discovered that it was a

foreign, frowned-upon language in the board rooms through which they were moving.

The senior levels of Irish business are occupied by people who intersperse 'portfolios' with 'suites' and 'key drivers' with 'value propositions' with an ease that suggests they have been doing it for years. A lot of 'driving' is also done by the decision-makers. Not driving as we know it, because that usually is left to the chauffeurs, but 'driving' efficiencies, profits, revenues, performance, margins and any other possible noun you can put the verb in front of which enhances the reputation of the chief.

And a little bit of research into the speaking patterns of chief executives is as much evidence as we need to support this view. Take Sir Anthony O'Reilly; we like him. Not because of his exploits for the Irish rugby team as a wing in a long and illustrius career, or because he runs a successful newspaper group. He just does jargon with a flourish, making it almost sound as if all the plain-speakers of the world are just not worthy. Take Sir Anthony's comments in a trading statement from Independent News and Media (INM) in November 2005:

> 2005 was a year of significant progress for Independent. We expanded our geographic reach and indicated that we are both language and location indifferent, provided the economic indices are favourable. We sharpened our strategic focus, continued to re-size our operations, and increased our financial flexibility.

This is one of those bits of jargon that does not lack meaning but contains the sort of expressions that make you wonder if there is a language consultant feeding public companies a whole set of new phrases so they can make what they are doing sound a bit more breathtaking.

The achievement of a condition of 'language and location' indifference with favourable 'economic indices' has an epic ring to it and sharpening the 'strategic focus' and 're-sizing' the operations makes the company's cost-cutting sound like a selfless humanitarian act.

Not for Sir Anthony the mundane business of INM merely 'buying' new titles either. In 2005, he described the company's purchase of a stake in Indian newspaper *Danik Jagran* as akin to 'entering a new theatre of strategic investment.' For a moment, you would be forgiven for mistaking it for an initiative in the 'war against terror'.

He was at it again in September 2006 at the publication of INM's interim results for the six months to the end of the previous June. His outlook statement began:

> INM's geographically diversified portfolio of market-leading assets, across diverse multi-media platforms, continues to underpin INM's clear and compelling international growth strategy.

Again, you sort of understand what he is getting at, but you just wonder if there was no translator around to enable us to make sense of it. I asked INM's chief in Ireland, Vincent Crowley, to translate it on the business news one morning. 'I think Sir Anthony puts it very well,' he responded. No breaking of ranks in senior INM management there, and a polite rebuff to yours truly on the extent of his knowledge of business terms, perhaps.

Kelly Martin, the soft-spoken chief executive officer of Irish pharmaceutical company Elan, has also made some notable contributions to the English language. In order that the company's drug Tysabri, used in the treatment of multiple sclerosis, be allowed return to market after the death of a patient in clinical trials, Martin looked forward to 'content-rich discussions' with the Food and Drug Administration in the United States.

The drinks industry is forever trying to present itself in a better light as it comes under attack from different quarters for shamelessly targeting young drinkers and luring them into the evils of consuming alcohol. Paul Walsh, chief executive officer of Diageo, the company that has Guinness and Smirnoff among its brands, came to the Irish Management Institute conference in County Wicklow determined to present his company as conscientious and prepared to make its contribution to any initiative aimed at targeting binge drinking.

So far so good, until Paul Walsh tried to put it all in words:

> I will argue that a real, embedded and strategic commit-
> ment to responsible behaviour – even if it appears
> superficially counter to a business's commercial
> interests – is actually a critical business enabler in the
> modern world of stakeholder advocacy.

And there was more:

> A modern business leader should treat social
> responsibility or responsible behaviour not as a tick-
> box hygiene factor, or a marketing exercise, but rather
> embrace it as a driver of long-term growth.

And there was even more:

> The complex societal nature of alcohol misuse is such
> that a multi-stakeholder, multi-action response is
> necessary to deliver long-term change.

And God bless cable company NTL Ireland, which was chuffed to tell us it had been taken over by Liberty Global Management. NTL took this opportunity to inform us that in Ireland, it has 370,000 'revenue-generating units'. It later confirmed that those revenue-generating units, were, indeed, what most people would describe as customers. Bank of Ireland told us in a statement in September 2006 that the job of its asset management services is to 'harness our global distribution platforms and build a portfolio of investment boutiques'.

Heady stuff, you agree? The group chief executive of Accenture caught our attention early in 2008 when he circulated an email to other senior executives at the company. Mark Foster begins by stating as his desire: '... wanting to give you continued visibility of our growth platform agenda', and then announces a significant name change: 'we are changing the name of the Human Performance service line to Talent & Organisation Performance, effective immediately.' He then explains the reasons for the change: 'With the rise of the multi-polar world, the task of finding and managing talent has become more complex, turbulent and contradictory than ever before.'

If you are not baffled at this stage, you can struggle on to the most remarkable part of Foster's statement. He says what must be done is to teach organisations to

> ... expand their talent management agenda from a
> narrow and tactical focus on human resources

activities around the employee life cycle to a broad and strategic focus on human resources activities around the life employee, to a broad and strategic focus on highly integrated systems of capabilities fundamental to business strategies and operations.

Phew!

So, there is no doubting the fact that the more senior you become in a company, the less clear your intentions are likely to appear. Maybe some of it stems from anxiety of being found out not to have what it takes to stay at senior levels, but surely no one could read the above and believe it to be an outstanding, nay, a competent contribution to the debate on people at work.

A name change also seems to have inspired a host of new words and concepts for the chiefs at the company that most of us knew in the past as Golden Pages:

> Golden Pages has recently changed its name to Truvo Ireland Limited. Truvo Ireland is the new name to fit our future development plans. The new company name reflects our rapidly evolving company. It echoes our rich heritage of leadership and innovation, our passion and commitment to our customers and our streamlined and intuitive new identity.

I do not know what 'Truvo' does to you, but the bold claims made about it leave me cold. A quick glance at its website provides no reassurance:

> The individuals that make up this company have a lot in common. We share goals, colleagues and customers.

We share passion, energy and commitment. We share the same vision. We are seeking bright, passionate, earnest, and committed individuals to join our team at Truvo Ireland. If you are customer oriented, flexible, a committed and passionate deliverer of promises and a 'feet-on-the-ground' sort of person, then why not look at some of the positions available here at Truvo Ireland and consider joining our team?

Yes, admittedly, not a difficult word in sight but the enthusiasm is enough to send you into a deep depression. Just what is a 'feet-on-the ground sort of person', for instance? Just don't let them see you jumping.

Even the book-selling business, where an appreciation of good language might be expected, has some jargon peddlers in its midst. Forecasting tough economic times ahead, Borders Group Chief Executive Officer, George Jones, had this to say:

We are pleased to have the confidence and backing of our largest shareholder, Pershing Square, which has agreed to provide funding that gives us adequate opportunity to implement our plans this year and pursue a range of longer term solutions through the strategic alternatives review process. We believe that consummation of the transactions under the commitment will make us fully funded for 2008, where absent these measures, liquidity issues may otherwise have arisen in the next few months.

The words bandied about by many business leaders suggest that plainness and simplicity are potentially life-threatening diseases, so whatever needs to be communicated must be achieved with a flourish to sweep customers and staff alike off their feet.

The fact that many of these companies are successful suggests that they know something we don't, but who says they could not be profitable with a bit of plain-speaking? It is worth a try.

Chapter 6
Talking Politics

Most of our politicians go into public life with their eyes wide open. But what about their mouths? There is a school of thought that says the bigger the fuss you make in politics, the more likely it is that, come the next election, you will find yourself without a seat to sit on. Seasoned politicians will remind younger colleagues that often the less said the better, and if you are going to do something, do it and don't say much about it in advance. I make these points to support my view that, today, the first casualty of modern politics is often plain English.

Given a choice, politicians, especially those in office, would prefer to inflict serious damage on the English language than take up a position that could alienate them from thousands of their constituents. It means that they spend half their time lunging for that popular place known as the 'middle ground'. Civil servants are on hand to ensure that not only do they find the 'middle ground', but that they are tethered to it in order to avoid any announcement that could be construed as making a hard and fast decision. Civil servants are at their most cautious when one of their political masters is asked to speak about that great old institution itself – the public service.

During 2006, the then Taoiseach, Bertie Ahern, was asked to make a speech on the topic of public sector reform. The civil servants who wrote the speech for him came up with the following ingenious way of getting him to say nothing.

A key challenge for the Public Service is to continue to justify public confidence in its ability to deliver. The Public Service needs to continually 'up its game', through a process of ongoing renewal so that it can confidently demonstrate its credentials on service delivery.

This is as meaningless as you can get, and riddled with the sort of expressions that make you wonder seriously about the thought process in the public service. If you kindly accept 'up its game' as a brief flirtation with plain English and understand what the author is getting at, you are thrown right back into chaos and confusion by the idea that the public service can 'confidently demonstrate its credentials on service delivery'.

The former Taoiseach sometimes attended events that carried themes that themselves were hard to understand. He headed out to Fingal County Council's new offices in Blanchardstown in May 2006 to launch Fingal Development Board's Strategy Reports – 'Strategy into Action – 2006–2008' and 'Connecting People, Places and Prosperity: An Economic Strategy for Fingal 2006–2011'.

The Taoiseach told his audience that he was conscious that it was the first time he had visited the new offices, but instead of settling for saying they were 'handsome', he described them as 'another manifestation of enhanced public service delivery'.

The hand of the same speech-writer was probably at work for the few words that Mr Ahern was asked to deliver at the opening of Hewlett-Packard's new video-conferencing technology in Leixlip in June 2006: 'As a result we are creating both the intellectual and the organisational capacity to meet the needs of the most forward-oriented companies, such as yours, across the key developmental industries'.

It is little wonder that with these complex constructions swimming around his brain, Mr Ahern used to lapse into some jargon of his own during unscripted moments. In May 2006, he criticised an unofficial action by train drivers in Cork and reminded the assembled media that there were 'extensive mechanisms available under industrial relations machinery'. Doesn't it sound just like a job for a mechanic?

The script-writers in the Department of the Taoiseach obviously have a direct line to their colleagues in the adjoining Department of Finance building. In his time there, present Taoiseach Brian Cowen was sent out to discuss the tightening of tax loopholes and the need for our economy to develop. He ended up providing us with a cliché-ridden assessment: 'We must therefore use this window of opportunity to transform our infrastructure to world-class standards'. We understood what he meant, but at this stage in their long lives, 'window of opportunity' and 'world class' are terms that really should be taken out of their misery.

The then Minister for Finance went on to tell us that there were certain initiatives we had to take to ensure that this infrastructure transformation took place: 'We must avoid the development of a narrow, localised mindset and try to ensure an integrated prioritised approach to regional development'.

In another ground-breaking speech, at the launch of an historic alliance between University College Dublin and the Institute of Bankers in Ireland, the minister introduced us to a new verb:

> The alliance will also well-serve the growing demand,
> from the industry, for applied and commercial research
> in banking and financial services.

There is some unexpected entertainment along the way. In 2006, the then Minister for the Environment, Dick Roche, looked forward to the 'roll-out of brown bins'. At last, we had found a good, green home for that noun that would appear to be everywhere, and has taken the place of 'introduce' and 'bring in'.

Yes, 'rolling out' has become one of the most popular pastimes in modern Irish politics. There are others, including 'considering the options', 'addressing all the issues' and 'exploring the possibilities'. These are all pursuits that politicians are familiar with, and it doesn't necessarily follow that they all culminate in the slightly more specific action of 'taking a decision'.

When the Minister for Education, Mary Hanafin, was asked in 2007 by my RTÉ colleague Ryan Tubridy about concerns about Internet 'addiction' among schoolchildren, the minister announced that she was developing a 'policy template'. In response to growing indiscipline in the classroom, the same minister announced the establishment of 'behaviour support teams'. Backing groups for the class dossers, we wondered?

Minister Hanafin's department came up with a plan to deal with under-performing teachers in early 2008, but made it clear that disciplinary action would not be triggered by 'sustained performance deficiencies'.

The same sort of thinking goes into announcements on other social issues, such as this one related to homelessness, unveiled by Minister of State Noel Ahern in May 2006:

> Our focus must be on long-term accommodation and the non-accommodation supports required to enable the people involved to move out of homelessness. In addition, my Department is currently in the course of preparing a revised and updated Government Strategy

on Homelessness. A key focus of the revised Strategy will be to ensure that all the needs of the homeless person are addressed with a view to enabling them to move out of emergency accommodation into more sustainable tenancy options at the earliest opportunity.

Just which wise man came up with the creation 'move out of homelessness'? The homeless, in most cases, have already 'moved out' and deserve a more human description of their plight. If confronted on the street with the information that they were going to be presented with 'more sustainable tenancy options', they would be forgiven for allowing their eyes to glaze over.

The Minister of State at the Office of Public Works, Tom Parlon, was sent out on *Morning Ireland* in 2006 to talk about a new website that gave town planners the information that they needed about places that were prone to flooding around the country. His opening remarks suggested that some OPW civil servant had left him with an explanation of the project that had not been dredged:

I set up a flood policy review group when I took over my responsibilities at the Office of Public Works and that basically in the end having consulted the agencies involved gave the OPW the lead with regard to flood relief in the future and as part of what is international best practice now that involves sort of risk management and in future avoiding the future increases of risk. It involves a very complex river catchment management risk policy that will be done in areas and involves non-structural and impact mitigation measures.

It is not really clear whether or not flood-prone households would find this sentence reassuring. My advice would be just to keep away from rivers, because by the time OPW policy is deciphered, you may have already been swept downriver. Tom Parlon is a farmer from County Offaly and on the occasions I have met him, I have never once heard him speak like this. But do ministers not have a duty to ask civil servants: 'What does this mean in English?'

The Department of Trade, Enterprise and Employment decided that it was time to publish an 'Action Plan' in 2005. One part of it dealt with how the agency that deals with Irish companies, Enterprise Ireland, was going to be organised. In a statement, it said that the then minister, Micheál Martin, had 'directed a complete business process and organisational re-engineering of Enterprise Ireland's overseas and marketing support division', and spoke of a joint working group that would ensure the 'most effective operationalisation of the Technology Ireland concept'. The plan went on to tell us that the 'internationalisation of Irish companies' would be the key agenda item in the coming year'. And there was more:

> Supports will be provided on an individual and group or cluster basis. Specifically, this will mean more intensive and pro-active use of sectoral and group interventions to jointly agree priorities and sectoral development agendas.

For those concerned that Enterprise Ireland was going to be transformed beyond recognition, the plan provided the comforting knowledge that the 'client offering' would continue to provide 'a customised, holistic approach to business development'.

And then we come to that agreement known as social partnership. In 1989, it all started with the Programme for National Recovery, an agreement signed between government, employers and trade unions, which amounted to a trade-off of industrial peace in return for modest wage increases for workers. Social partnership has been seen as a great success, and is widely viewed to have been partly responsible for the economic success enjoyed, especially in the last ten years. It may be a successful concept but it has yet to be evaluated for its contribution to the English language. And that may not be a bad thing at all.

The latest social partnership agreement, reached in the middle of 2006 was known as 'Towards 2016'. It took months to negotiate, but clearly those negotiations didn't involve discussing its title. Indeed, exhaustion may have set in before the participants got around to naming the thing, but whatever the excuse, it raises questions.

One thing we can be sure of: 'Away From 2016' was not a runner. Perhaps, the more alliterative 'Towards 2016 Together' got on to the short list. We are told by its authors that 2016 is a 'historically significant date' – the centenary of 1916 – but that doesn't excuse the sheer meaningless of 'Towards 2016' as conveying anything but the fact that we are all headed towards there whether we like it or not.

We would forgive a limp title if the content of that latest social partnership agreement was uplifting. But it isn't. No, it is full of waffle and dreary words. The preamble by the then Taoiseach, Mr Ahern, said that the agreement would focus on 'the needs of children, young adults, people of working age, older people and people with disabilities'. Would 'everyone' not have covered it? He also told us partnership had worked partly because it had promoted a 'culture of dialogue' and offered the best way forward by 'providing an important and strategic framework for meeting the economic and social challenges ahead'.

Moving from the preamble to the introduction to 'Towards 2016' itself and concepts such as 're-inventing and repositioning Ireland's social policies', 'deepening capabilities' and a 'joined-up policy approach' then make their entrance. It says that 'departments and agencies will need to work closely with the social partners and others to become networks that undertake delivery, outreach and analysis effectively'.

We knew that we should have left it there but a document that contained so many quirky ideas in its introduction aroused our curiosity and we just had to delve further. The document is littered with mentions of the 'life cycle approach'. Page 11 provides the explanation:

> 'The life cycle approach adopts the perspective of the citizen as the centrepiece of building a new social policy approach, within this ten-year framework agreement. The key lifecyle phases include children, people of working age, older people and people with disabilities. Chapter 3 of this agreement sets out the key goals and strategies across these key phases for the provision of three critical and overlapping types of interventions identified by NESC [National Economic and Social Council]: key services, income supports and activation measures new and innovative responses.

Always be suspicious about any document that offers 'new and innovative' responses because the necessity for saying the same thing twice is never very clear. The 'lifecycle approach' adopted by the authors, by the way, 'offers the potential of a more streamlined outcomes-focused approach'. Indeed, the 'implementation of the lifecycle group approach' appears to be the main aim of the report as you struggle through all 141 pages of it.

Those of you not prepared to take our word for it, and wishing to give the contents of 'Towards 2016' the benefit of the doubt, need look no further than its embrace of new technology on page 57:

> The eInclusion Stakeholders Group will develop, implement, communicate and monitor progress on a new national eInclusion strategy which will address those in each lifecycle stage that are digitally excluded.

Did nobody shout stop? Was there no one involved in this partnership process who read this and let out a cry of anguish? Was an editor not consulted? Was the Army not brought in, for God's sake? Does this sentence not seriously bring into question the state of mind of some of the people running the country? Just who exactly are the 'digitally excluded'? Oh, yes, they could have said they would be helping out those who had no Internet access or computers but, hey, we would all have understood that.

And, no, it wasn't a temporary blip. Page 87 out of what was now becoming 'Towards the Death of the English Language' gave us an insight into what the participants in this partnership process had agreed:

> The parties are also agreed on the need for a subsequent review of the workplace learning and

upskilling offerings available, especially from the point of view of user friendliness/modularisation, the provision of generic, transferable as well as sector specific skills; future skills requirements; geographical accessibility; cost; and means of activation.

Is this English? If so, who was the teacher? And what was his or her motive? Staunch defenders of this social partnership process or 'framework', or whatever they wish to call it, will point to its success in bringing us to where we are today. Yes, but did they have to destroy a language along the way? Is it not time the 'digitally excluded' got their fingers out and revolted?

Mind you, no Irish politician has come near the jargon heights reached by the current British Prime Minister, Gordon Brown, when he sought to put his policy positions forward even before the Labour Party began its uninterrupted 11 years in power. Back in 1994, he spoke of the virtues of 'post neo-classical endogenous growth theory'. His peculiar way with words did not prevent him from making it all the way to No. 10 Downing Street, although he may have left some people confused along the way.

Then, there is Europe and the damage it is inflicting on us, which does provide sceptics with fertile ground. A proposal from the European Commission to establish a European Institute of Technology was circulated in 2006 and contained what one listener to *The Business* described as a 'verbal jargon-ridden comfort zone of "critical masses", "best resources", "worldwide attractiveness", "integration of the knowledge triangle", "boundary spanning skills", and "support geographical, cross-sectoral and inter-disciplinary mobility of skills and resources".' Former member of the British Labour Government and EU

Commissioner Peter Mandelson had this take on one element of the negotiations on a World Trade Organisation deal a couple of years ago:

> We could limit the permitted upward variation, so as to prevent a below formula cut in one or several lines being offset by 'piling' the shortfall all into a disproportionate cut in another single line. If we could limit recourse to flexibility around the linear cut to a limited number of tariffs ...

Those who bemoan the fact that the circumstances of people living in many parts of the developing world have not changed that much over the last 20 years can use Mandelson's language to explain just why things may not be clicking into place in some countries.

Chapter 7
Stark Warnings

I nearly managed to write a whole book on the subject of clichés and jargon without getting to discuss that profession whose very existence depends on the ability to say much the same thing in many different ways as often as possible.

Yes, we journalists, though we may think ourselves direct descendants of some of the great literary figures of the

18th, 19th and early 20th centuries, have a reliance on the sort of language that is neither easy on the ear nor graceful on the eye. My conscience would not allow me to write a book about crimes committed against the English language without referring to some of the patterns of speech and prose that my journalistic colleagues and I like to consider to be our 'tools of the trade'.

Let me be honest about this. I am a sinner, even though I set out with the best of intentions. Hence the accusing looks of colleagues when I emerge from the RTÉ Radio studio having uttered such obscenities as 'exited the business', 'bring to market', 'negatived', and 'harmonisation of relations'. (This last one my son pulled me up on: I docked him his pocket money.)

Having owned up to my own frailties, I think it only right that I point out that the Irish media is home to some strange terms that may not match the efforts of our business people, but do suggest that we are in need of some remedial work ourselves.

A colleague recently introduced an item on the new Metro that has been planned to run from Dublin city centre to Dublin Airport as having received a 'generally broad welcome'. Work that one out if you can. It bellows 'caution'.

I may be exaggerating a touch, but most of the reports produced by consultants in the last four or five years criticising a public service, or the way, for instance, a bank treats its customers, have been described as 'damning indictments' by nearly every journalist covering the story. Because it is now widely used shorthand, what exactly the report is a 'damning indictment' of is rarely included. In crime stories, why do the media tend to describe the victim or culprit as being 'named locally as…'. Is it the locals we don't trust and do we need to see the passport first before taking their word for it?

We love and embrace every 'war of words'. The war is usually 'sparked'. Of course, it is only an argument between rival politicians but that does not convey the drama, does it? If the 'war of words' persists, we love telling our audience that the two combatants are on a 'collision course'. To get a row going, some statement or action will often 'ignite the touch-paper', leading to far greater consequences.

If we want to speculate on the outcome of a disagreement, difficulty or dispute, it is no longer sufficient for us to rule nothing out. No, we must make it clear that 'nothing can be ruled in or out'.

In our search for greater public interest, we shall never be satisfied with a prison governor issuing a 'warning' about overcrowding in his jail. No, it will have to be a 'stark warning'. We have abused the word 'tragedy' so much that it can appear in a sentence bemoaning the fate that has befallen our local football team being relegated as often as it can appear where it belongs – to describe an event where loss of life or serious personal injury has occurred. And in a similar vein, we shall tell of someone 'losing their fight for life' when 'died' says the same thing without the cliché.

We shall report on 'new initiatives' without stopping to think that it cannot be an initiative if it is not new. We ape our friends in business by reporting on 'new and innovative' ways of doing things. Reports or studies due to be published are 'eagerly anticipated' or 'eagerly awaited'. They will no doubt be 'wide-ranging'. They will sometimes contain a 'package of measures' and cover a 'range of issues'. They will be 'warmly welcomed' by some, and 'vehemently opposed' or 'coolly received' by others. They could conceivably turn out to be 'bombshells' or, at the other end of the scale, they may turn out to be 'damp squibs'. Some of the reports, although this happens rarely enough, will point that overused digit – the 'finger of blame'. And, just in case our bosses do not get it, we will always attach the adjective 'key' as in key findings, or key reports, to our efforts. John Humphrys, in his delightful book *Lost for Words* lists some of the clichés that his BBC Radio 4 listeners find most offensive. They include:

Grinds to a halt
At the end of the day
On the back burner
On the ground
On the back foot
On hold
Up for grabs
Moment of truth
A question mark hangs over
Conspicuous by his absence
Hail of bullets
Shrouded in mystery
Calm before the storm
Explore every avenue
Leave no stone unturned

We are familiar with them all and there are plenty more to remind us that the cliché disease is not one unique to the media in Britain. Just think of how we try to build the suspense. If we get tired of talking of 'question marks hanging over', we will happily invoke the weather and talk about 'a cloud of uncertainty'. Yes, the first rule of modern journalism is never to be afraid of a bit of exaggeration. That is why the adjective 'major' appears on more front pages and is uttered by more broadcasters and reporters on radio and television than there are fish in the sea, or pebbles on the beach, or whichever metaphor takes your fancy. Just see what attaching the adjective 'minor' does to your career prospects.

We have all signed up for the preposition change, too. We gladly tell our audience that the minister is committed to doing something 'around the issue' of classroom discipline, when doing something 'about it' would surely be a far more onerous political challenge. The funding that he or she provides for the initiative we happily present as a 'cash injection' and if we have to mention it being paid in 'tranches', so be it. As for negotiations, they in themselves are not sufficient to arouse the interest of listeners, viewers, readers or our editors.

All talks and negotiations must at the very least be 'crucial', possibly 'crunch' and if the editor still isn't paying any attention to our overtures at that stage, we can always promote them to 'make or break' or 'last ditch' status. Doubtless, you won't be asked what exactly those self-same talks will make or break. Talks are never long; no, they have to be 'protracted'. We take 'initiatives' more often than we take vitamins. 'Breakthrough' is so overused that it is difficult to work out whether or not it actually means anything any more.

We are also gleeful in our rush to describe what some of our news-making friends do. For trade unions, there is no greater thrill for a shop steward and his or her colleagues than to hear the industrial action they are taking described as 'putting down a marker'. If you are an employer who has not been paying a fair and reasonable wage to your workers, you are involved in that new sporting contest – a 'race to the bottom'. We nod approvingly when we attend press conferences and allow central bankers to tell us that the Irish housing market has undergone a 'correction' and that what we are witnessing is a 'soft landing'.

We also live in a world where the people making news around us are delivering 'wake-up calls', looking for 'sea changes' and warning that their particular gripe is no less than a 'time bomb waiting to go off'. Just think pensions on that one, and think about the number of times you have heard people say in the last six months that the hole in our pensions fund is, you guessed it, a 'time bomb' waiting to go off. Or is that 'ticking'?

We will happily describe any organisation that provides us with regular dollops of advice on a particular matter as a 'think-tank'. Tanks that think, in other words, and so out of date and unhelpful that they should be banished. For an even more exhaustive list of overused clichés that journalists should seriously avoid, the 'stale expressions' section of Harold Evans' bible *Essential English* is required reading. Among the ones he lists are:

> Acid test
> All walks of life
> Burning issue
> Crack troops
> Daring daylight robbery
> Drew a line
> Inextricably linked
> Pros and cons
> Sweeping changes

There are plenty more, and Evans' book also does a service to journalists by listing the much more straightforward versions of terms that we should use instead of those that are more laboured.

When we say that the gardaí are 'following a definite line of enquiry', do we stop and ask ourselves if this means anything any more? As journalists we love 'throwing down gauntlets', 'firing broadsides' and 'shots across bows'.

If people are reluctant to talk, we tell the public that they are 'tight-lipped'. And then there is reporting from war zones; fighting is always 'fierce', as if we would ever think it was going to be 'delicate'; and like a light switch, situations can move from 'tense' to 'calm'; and the government coming under pressure from its former military allies to get the hell out of the presidential palace is in all cases 'beleaguered', it seems.

In defence of my own profession, could it be said that most of the audience understands what is being said or hinted at in most of these hackneyed and clichéd expressions? No, there can be no immunity or exemptions from the use of plain English. What effort would it take to replace 'tight-lipped' with 'they are saying nothing at the moment' and a 'definite line of enquiry' with 'they are making good progress in finding the culprit'? Not too difficult, is it? We can also move beyond the breathlessness that has every disagreement or dispute threatening the future of the universe. Fewer clichés, more facts.

Chapter 8
Bad Health

One of the big political initiatives of the early 21st century in Ireland was the decision by the Minister for Health, Mary Harney TD, to scrap eight health boards around the country and replace them with an agency known as the Health Service Executive.

Four years on, the state of Ireland's health service remains the subject of endless debate, with many taking the view that the 'big change' has not brought with it the improvements for which many people were hoping. We leave others to adjudicate on that particular debate. However, from the perspective of this author, one of the great failings of the HSE has been its inability to communicate to patients, taxpayers and, indeed, its political masters in a language that might be easily understood.

Instead, it has adopted what can only be described as 'consultant' speak, which might be excusable in some businesses or industries but surely cannot be tolerated in a service where life, death and well-being are the main considerations.

In 2005, the HSE chose to employ business consultants Tribal Secta to analyse the overcrowding that existed in the accident and emergency departments of our hospitals. This 'outsourcing' took place despite the presence in our hospitals of hundreds of people who surely must have had some expertise themselves in working out what the difficulties were. Whatever the motivation, Tribal Secta did its consulting and produced a report that contained insights such as this:

This marries with international thinking on improving emergency waits and flows which has converged around, for example, improvements in the management demand to departments, effective patient flow and management whilst in the department, appropriate staffing and interventions, reducing duplication and employing lean thinking in care process re-design.

And there was more:

The a and e crisis in Ireland, as with other countries around the world, is not uni-factorial. The causes of increased attendances and waits around the country are rather multi-factorial, taking into account forces and drivers in a wide range of areas from finance, demographics, social and radical change, health system operation and workforce, to changing expectations from ourselves as consumers on all aspects of service delivery.

It may pain you to know that these business consultants got very well paid for telling us, among other things, that the problem of hundreds of our patients spending too much time on trolleys in Accident and Emergency was related to the absence of 'lean thinking in care process re-design'. So, being the generous types we are, we put the blame firmly at the door of the business consultants themselves in coming up with these gems of jargon. Surely the HSE itself contained people of a much simpler frame of mind, we said to ourselves.

But, thanks to some 'tip-offs' from listeners to *The Business*, we discovered that the jargon disease was alive and well and infecting the HSE like a super bug. One listener, Aidan Thomas, looked for some information about something called the Winter Initiative after reading about it in the *Evening Herald*. Using his initiative, he looked up the HSE website to find out exactly what it was and came across the following:

> The key feature of the Winter Initiative is that it is not an accountable delivery unit. It is a corporate co-ordinating mechanism to facilitate the accountable pillars working together to put in place and monitor implementation of the various elements of the plan.

Wow! A spokesperson for the HSE Communications office accepted that the description was 'a little verbose and long-winded' and offered this somewhat clearer explanation:

> Basically, this particular sentence means that the Winter Initiative is not a specific new section of the HSE. It is a plan which aims to co-ordinate the activities of several areas of the HSE such as hospitals, nursing homes and community settings to ensure that all areas of the HSE are pulling in the same direction in order to provide the best possible care to patients during a time when demand on the health services is high.

The HSE also promised to put what it called a 'jargon-buster' on its website which will clearly explain any unfamiliar or technical terms in future.

But there is more work to be done. Mary in Blanchardstown was good enough to post us in a copy of the HSE's transformation plan 2007–2010. I immediately put down the thriller I was reading and plunged into this glossy, green brochure. Admittedly, the mention of 'simplified patient journeys' as one of the 'six priorities' of the plan set the alarm bells ringing but I decided to persevere.

This transformation plan contained some truly remarkable goals, none of which we understood. Here's a sample:

> Develop integrated end-to-end patient/client journey processes.
>
> Implement a national model for multi-disciplinary patient centred care delivery.
>
> Develop and implement shared care service packages.
>
> Implement sector specific service transformation, consistent with integrated PCCC configuration framework.

Other projects to which the HSE commits itself are a 'migration strategy for procurement transactional processes into national shared services' and the 'development of an information governance framework for clinical and demographic data sharing'. Now, maybe everyone working in the health service understands all these concepts and we are doing them a great disservice by suggesting otherwise. However, our hunch is that they do not.

The same cavalier approach to plain English is evident in the early efforts of a new agency in the health service. The Health Information and Quality Agency, which goes by the acronym, HIQA – sounds like HikWah – has been given the job of making sure that standards of service are high in our hospitals. One of

HIQA's first tasks was to carry out a 'hygiene audit' of our hospitals, and the report published on this subject contained such insights as 'we will work with the HSE and others to develop a national suite of performance indicators aimed at focussing improvement in the areas most needed'. This is no isolated lapse. In the remainder of that report, there is a sprinkling of terms that would be more often seen in a business manual. HIQA's literature is littered with references to 'driving improvements', 'engaging stakeholders', making 'robust arrangements' and 'managing change'.

'The Authority will expect the HSE to performance manage the respective hospitals against the implementation of these recommendations,' is just another sample of HIQA's way with words from a recently published report.

One senior official with the HSE in the south-west tried to explain a local staffing problem on radio in early 2008 and treated us to a range of expressions from 'working through the process' to 'amend the skill mix accordingly' to 'scope out the various challenges'.

We have also discovered that 'integrated care pathways' have become popular among health service managers. Would it require a visit to the local DIY store to put them in place, I wondered?

Amid our chuckles about the language being written, and the words being spoken by the managers of the health service, and the managers' obvious need for some lessons in plain English, we did ask ourselves if there was something more worrying at work here. And we came to the conclusion that jargon could hide a lot of inadequacies when it came to providing a proper health service. Medical consultants have been under pressure to transform their bedside manner in recent years so that patients are no longer left in the dark about what is wrong with them. So perhaps it is time that the HSE itself takes a long hard look at its own efforts to communicate. It would be nice to know what we are being told, warts and all, without having to consult a dictionary on jargon. Plain English is the best prescription.

Chapter 9
Fighting Back

Promoters of plain English could be forgiven for feeling a little like Hans Brinker, the young boy who reputedly put his finger in the dyke in Holland in a vain attempt to keep back the flood waters. No sooner does it appear that progress is being made in dealing with our very own linguistic flood than along

comes some politician or chief executive to puncture a hole in our optimism.

Aer Lingus's chief executive, Dermot Mannion, sprinkles his interviews with mentions of 'going forward' and tells us that certain initiatives are a 'win-win all round'. The former Tánaiste, Mary Harney TD, normally a plain talker, tells us that she is 'driving change' in the health service and highlights the need for a 'bells and whistles' service. Bank of Ireland Private Banking advertises 'outstanding opportunities for exceptional individuals'. They are looking for people who 'have the ambition and energy to push boundaries and reach new heights' and want applicants who 'enjoy relationship building and bringing their personality to work'. So do not apply if you intend on leaving 'your personality' at home then.

There are other worrying signs. Recently, the clergy appears to have got the bug. The Capuchin Franciscans were looking for recruits to the priesthood and had posters on the LUAS light rail service in Dublin bearing the message 'Live the dream and make a difference.'

Not to be outdone, in May 2005, the Catholic Archdiocese of Dublin advertised for a Human Resources Director. The advertisement, placed by their recruiters, PriceWaterhouse Coopers, was low on spiritual content and high on jargon:

> This appointment will entail the establishment of a HR function which will ensure that HR strategies developed are effectively aligned with organisational objectives and processes from both compliance and developmental perspectives. The appointee will be committed to developing and promoting 'best practice' in supporting all employees to maximise their potential

in the achievement of organisational goals. At the same time he/she will provide leadership in devising imaginative and innovative Human Resource programmes which will have a strategic impact on the mission of the Diocese. Candidates for the position will be experienced, mature and qualified human resource professionals with superior leadership skills and a proven management track record. The appointee will be practiced in the management of organisational change and experienced in working at board, policy, strategic and operational levels.

Dublin City Council is also doing its best to ensure that no plain English interferes with its daily operations. Its street cleaners have become 'hygiene specialists' and the dreaded clampers travel around in vans bearing the ominous message: 'This vehicle may be used to facilitate the immobilisation of illegally parked vehicles.'

What does the recruitment arm of consultants KPMG mean when it says that successful applicants for a job in one of its client companies will have to have 'international mobility'? Does it mean they will need a passport? Why do so many companies become instant astronauts by operating 'in that space'? Why does Fianna Fáil Minister Martin Cullen feel the need to tell us he is 'solutions-driven' when any other political ambition would be a bit puzzling?

Why do trade union officials tend to 'explore avenues'? What about 'parks' and 'crescents'? Just what did occupational psychologists Pearn Kandola have in mind when they carried out a survey and focused on people who were 'technically competent but people incompetent'.

Car-makers remain shameless devotees of gobbledygook. Lexus tried to woo new car buyers with this description of one its new models:

> Even at rest the new RX350 exudes an unmistakable aura of dynamism, tempered with elegance, grace and a reassuring sense of composed strength. Once inside, the luxurious quality of the interior, coupled with the intelligent technology at your fingertips, envelops you with a feeling of unimaginable tranquillity.

When it's not cars, its trains, as this award-winning notice for passengers at Coleraine Train Station in Northern Ireland explains:

> Every Autumn a combination of leaves on the line, atmospheric conditions and prevailing damp conditions lead to a low adhesion between the rail head and the wheel which causes services to be delayed or even cancelled. NI Railways are committed to minimising service delays, where we can, by implementing a comprehensive low adhesion action programme.

A solicitors' firm in Dublin which subscribes to a British legal journal thought seriously about ending the subscription after the journal featured an advertisement for the 'Third Knowledge and Content' conference in July 2006. It offered a 'masterclass' in 'harvesting knowledge – capturing knowledge in narrative form "in the field under fire", "understanding and measuring the role of experience and experiential knowledge", and "getting young people to use knowledge from previous generations, reinterpreting the past in the context of their contribution to the potentialities of the future" and "creating social networks utilising the capability of informal networks for knowledge transfer and learning".'

A listener to *The Business* sent us a transcript of the first few words of a conference call. They were uttered by a senior vice-president in a company with its headquarters in the United States:

> We have to execute on our vision and leverage partner artifacts while implementing standard methodologies to deliver laser focused customer solutions.

Back at home, the *Professional Ireland* email newsletter carried comments from Michael Kelly, chief executive and president of Fineos, who said: 'Companies that are struggling to achieve straight-through processing by automating back-end functionality originating in front-office applications will especially benefit from this release'. The Institute of Chartered Accountants tried to lure members of the profession to a new masters' course in corporate leadership at Dublin City University. It offered, among other things, 'horizontal rather than functional perspectives on business'. Getting laid instead of laid off, perhaps? The recruitment pages of Ireland's newspapers continue to offend. Medical research companies like Slendertone shatter our illusions that progress is being made towards plainer English when they advertise for a Marketing Director:

> You have proven global or pan-European multi-channel marketing experience at senior executive level. Self-starting, you 'own your own results' and understand the difference between a stand-alone business

and a large corporation. Incisive as well as decisive, but also a team-player, you can fit into an inclusive 'first among equals' regime with a 'can-do' attitude. Bright and imaginative, you have 'your finger on the creative pulse' and can 'imagineer' [sic] future customer demand in terms of product development and translate that into sales figures.

But even the above could be categorised as literature of sorts when set against the internal ad for a 'general manager, wealth management' at ACC Bank. This is a crushing blow. It reminds us of the task facing us:

Actively engage throughout the organisation to reflect your personal encouragement, promotion and support for the development of the right capability, motivation and culture across the organisation which will be evidenced by the clear assignment of the right levels of accountability responsibility being taken in your areas of functional responsibility.

A customer of eircom gets worried when he is asked to send a prepaid envelope back to the company's 'Customer Suppression Department'. 'One begins to look askance at the eircom van parked down the street. Is it the suppression squad? Do they have me under scrutiny? Will I be bundled into that innocent-looking van as I walk past in a scene reminiscent of *The Day of the Jackal* and be spirited off to some remote exchange where I will spend the rest of my life bundling local loops?'

A spokesman for the company reassures him that it is a technical term and will see him being removed from one of those hellish marketing mailing lists. 'This is not our finest hour in communicating to our customers,' the spokesman confesses.

Dr Rory O'Donnell, Director of the National Economic and Social Council, describes the growing number of immigrants coming to Ireland as a 'very significant factor in driving the demographic trajectory in Ireland'. That 't' word is certainly popular. A note from Davy Stockbrokers highlights AIB's 'impairment trajectory'. Yes, it sounds painful.

Everywhere we look there is plenty of evidence that, far from promoting plain English, some individuals and agencies are hell-bent on making life even more confusing for all of us. Has it become the 'unwinnable war'? Should we despair? Is it time to accept that there is no going back and that with the passage of time, spoken and written English will become more and more complex? We hope not.

We want to appeal to you now to take up arms for this important cause. Your first job is to identify those 'tell-tale' signs that suggest someone is getting the 'gobbledygook' habit. The wrongdoers will generally say 'challenging' when they mean they have big, big problems. They will describe the performance of the company they run as 'robust' when they mean the liquidator in on his way to the premises in a taxi. Another sign is the replacement of the preposition 'about' with 'around'. This is one of the clearest symptoms and should at least merit a phone call to the nearest available helpline. When you hear a politician promising some action 'around the issue of teenage binge drinking', do not hold your breath.

Other worrying signs to look out for are the use of words such as 'traction', 'granularity', 'template', and 'systemic'. I have a dream, to quote Martin Luther King, that one day, there will be a backlash, a revolution, and that the public will decide not to vote for politicians because they speak in an unfamiliar language. This new era will see senior managers being demoted because they use the expressions 'driving change' and 'step change' too frequently at meetings. The day will surely dawn when RTÉ loses half its licence fee because its creative people persist in inviting staff members to brainstorming sessions at which they are expected to at the same time 'think outside the box' and 'tick the right boxes'.

In this new age, Ladybird books will be in great demand as business manuals, consultants' reports and political speeches are burnt at the stake. Yes, a fitting punishment for being 'stakeholders'.

Back in the real world, and in the absence of any hard evidence to the contrary, I would be pretty sure that none of these things will come to pass. In the meantime, I appeal to people to do their own bit to prevent the contamination of the English language. Never be afraid to ask a simple question. Never be afraid to query a word or phrase you do not understand. Do not use a six-syllable word where something much shorter and clearer is at hand. Above all, never make presumptions about what your audience, be it five or five hundred, does or does not understand.

We should not lose heart. We must get people out of this habit of using words and expressions that convey very little, if any, meaning. The good news is that there are organisations in our midst doing their best to hold back the gobbledygook invaders.

Not everyone is prepared to take the mangling of the English language lying down. The National Adult Literacy Agency (NALA) comes to it from a very simple perspective. It wants people to be able to understand what they are reading, and not just people with low literacy skills.

So, since 2004, the Agency has published a number of plain English guides to assist people. Three have been produced at this stage, dealing with legal terms, medical terms and financial services terms. The Agency hosts courses for managers in companies and provides a service whereby it scans the content of booklets before they are published. 'Staff taking part in these courses generally agree that what we are telling them makes sense, but they doubt if their senior managers will get the message when they go back to work. There is no doubt that some senior management would view plain English as a dumbing-down,' says the Agency's Plain English co-ordinator, Clodagh McCarthy.

The Financial Regulator, the state agency that regulates the activities of building societies, banks, credit unions, insurance companies and other financial services, was itself the victim of jargon in the early days of its existence.

The legislation that brought it into being decided that it should carry the name 'Independent Financial Services Regulatory Authority'. If that was not bad enough, some well-intentioned public official in the Central Bank decided that it might make more sense and be more manageable if it became known by the acronym IFSRA.

One of the great shocks to hit the financial services industry in Ireland in 2004 was a survey carried out by the self-same IFSRA that showed that 99 per cent of people did not know what IFSRA meant – in its acronym form or in its previous full-length form.

A year later, the collective brains of the Central Bank were applied to the job and the new term, Financial Regulator, was born. Since then, the Regulator has spent a lot of time not only explaining to people what it does but also ensuring that the literature that it publishes, and that is published by the banks and building societies it regulates, is easier to understand.

In addition to using the services of NALA, the Financial Regulator has also begun training its own staff in the use of plain English. Staff have been sent to Britain to take part in the only third-level course available in plain English in the United Kingdom and Ireland – a diploma course in London.

The Financial Regulator has itself changed its approach to what constitutes simply understood English by revising brochures with more illustrations and less text.

The woman leading the charge for simpler English, the Regulator's Consumer Director Mary O'Dea, takes the charitable view that banks do not purposely set out to complicate and to confuse their customers. She says that much of what they publish must, of necessity, be vetted by a legal department whose job it is not to make every word understandable, but to ensure that the financial services provided by the bank are legal. Mary O'Dea also says that some new entrants to the banking market in Ireland now realise that there is a strong business case for providing their customers with everything in plain English:

> They are making a virtue out of the fact that everything they do with their customers is straightforward and easily understood and that they do not go in for stuff that no one understands. Their own research has obviously told them that this sort of approach is good for business.

Perhaps the best hope for the world of business transforming itself into an oasis of plain English is the growing awareness that customers must be convinced of the merits of a service before they avail of it, and explaining it to them is a good start.

So great vigilance is required if we are truly to tackle the malaise of jargon and cliché-ridden prose and speeches. We should not become downhearted or defeatist, and we must realise that a greater good is served if we all make things easier for everyone to understand. And we do have our champions. Ryanair chief executive, Michael O'Leary, might not be everyone's cup of tea, but he is a wonderfully plain speaker and I have yet to come away from one of his press conferences feeling confused about the message he was trying to send.

This clamour for plain English is not some 'anti-intellectual' crusade either. A study carried out by Dr Daniel Oppenheimer at Princeton University, entitled 'Consequences of Erudite Vernacular Utilized Irrespective of Necessity: Problems with Using Long Words Needlessly', showed that the more straightforward the language used by the writer, the higher the writer's intelligence as rated by readers:

> It's important to point out that this research is not about problems with using long words but about using long words needlessly. If the best way to say something involves using a complex word, then by all means do so. But if there are several equally valid ways of expressing your ideas, you should go with the simpler one.

As I mentioned at the beginning of this book, it is not as if there are thousands of people who are deliberately setting out to confuse people. But there are too many people who think it acceptable that the language be spoken and written in a way that often hides the truth and promotes vagueness. We shall never live in a jargon-free world, but every policy-maker, broadcaster, journalist, public speaker, author, commentator, business person, and opinion-former can achieve some good by putting plain English at the centre of all they do and ensuring that whatever message they wish to send is one that is understood by as many people as possible. Go on – be simple and plain and make the English-speaking world a clearer place.

The A-Z of Jargon and Clichés

The use of jargon and clichés in the English language is growing all the time, so it's difficult to prepare a lexicon and be confident that it contains all the obscenities contained in written and spoken English today. Despite that, we have tried to give as comprehensive a list as possible of the most widely used and abused words and terms. We apologise in advance for omissions.

THAT'S NOT A LEARNING CURVE, AL — IT'S A BEGINNER'S SLOPE.

Tom Mathews.

Accountability

The word has lost most of its meaning through overuse. It is regularly used by politicians who are on the opposition benches to criticise the policies of their rivals in government. It is part of a trio of words that has become popular in Irish politics in the last decade – 'openness, transparency and accountability'.

Action

This is one of the really horrible verbs of modern business. 'To action' something is supposed to mean to do something.

Additionality

One of the favourite words of the former Minister for Transport, Martin Cullen, and used to describe a policy or initiative that is being extended or expanded.

Addressing the issue

This is a popular pastime of politicians, and is specifically designed to give the impression that something is being done without the promise of action. It is frequently interchanged with 'considering all options'.

Agencification

Some governments around the world, including our own, have become fond of setting up agencies to deal with political problems that were proving difficult to solve under old structures. This horrid word describes that process.

Around

This straightforward preposition has been hijacked, especially in spoken English, and has taken the place of the much more precise preposition 'about'. For example, politicians will frequently tell an audience they are doing some work 'around an issue', as distinct from 'about a particular issue'.

Astro-turfing
Where a person or organisation fakes 'grass-roots' support for their product on the Internet. Think hotel review websites where the 'guests' tell of their 'out of this world' experiences.

At the end of the day
Officially, the end of the day is midnight, but that does not stop thousands of business people from using it loosely as a preface to any particular remark they wish to make on almost any subject.

At this moment in time
In the same category as 'going forward', this expression is the crutch of those who just cannot think at that moment in time just what they wish to say. 'Now' would be better.

Avenues
Not the tree-lined variety, but the places beloved of the trade union movement. No agreement can be struck with anyone nowadays without all the avenues being explored.

Back-end loaded
On first reading, this sounds painful, but some research reveals that it is used to describe the performance of companies, many in the construction sector, which tend to become more profitable as the year progresses. In other words, they make more money towards the end of the year.

Bandwidth

It started out life as a term related to radio frequencies but, oh, how its role has been developed to mean space or room to do something. 'Have we got the bandwidth?' is a regular question for senior business people.

Baseball

Ninety-seven per cent of the Irish population may not know the rules of baseball, but the sport does deserve an award for the propagation of jargon. From 'stepping up to the plate', to 'touching base', to 'out in left field', one wonders would the world of business survive at all if it were not for those bulked-up men wielding their wooden bats.

Bells and whistles

The new way of saying 'with frills' – straight out of the USA.

Benchmarking

Irish public servants will be only too aware of the meaning of 'benchmarking'. It was most recently used to compare their responsibilities with those in equivalent positions in the private sector. Critics say it actually meant 'money for nothing' and that no benches got marked at all at all.

BER

A newish acronym which, spelled out, tells us that something is Beyond Economic Repair. My daughter dragged me down to the local mobile phone store when her Nokia went on the blink. The shop assistant – or was he called a 'senior customer care representative'? – shook his head and said the device was BER. Yes, she got a new one.

Best-of-breed

A description normally reserved for the sales ring at Goffs but many are the IT products or services that carry this label today. It is usually preceded by 'end-to-end' and followed by 'solutions'. It means 'top quality'.

Best-of-class

This is a first cousin of 'best-of-breed' and has nothing to recommend it. Simply 'the best' will do.

Best practice

One of the great puzzles of the twenty-first century is just what is best practice? Admittedly, it is not quite as impressive as 'international best practice'. Times and methods change so rapidly in this modern world that it is a dangerous test to be applying anyway.

Big picture

It is easy to visualise it: boss at the top of the table, urging his managers to look beyond their own responsibilities at the 'big picture'. Rarely will the said chief executive officer be able to define what the 'big picture' is, but better to throw it out as a challenge to his minions rather than come across all dull, eh? In this era of almost full employment, it is also a vital attribute for all job-seekers to be able to focus on the 'big picture'. We could stop all this nonsense at once by asking those who use the term what exactly it means. Blank stares guaranteed.

Big ticket item

This is the idea that stands out, the centrepiece of some initiative or other that should have the listening audience gasping in wonder at the sheer scale of it.

Blame-storm

A smart new name for a review process which usually ends up with someone being fingered for making a big mistake.

Bleeding edge

It sounds painful but it is the term used, particularly in the world of IT, to describe how a company has developed technology that is too far ahead of the market and, therefore, not workable for the time being. In other words, it's one step beyond 'leading edge'.

Blue sky thinking

This is a first cousin of strategic thinking, although a bit loftier. It is a nephew of 'thinking outside the box' and has yet to become commonplace in Ireland.

Boil the ocean

This means trying not to be too ambitious, i.e., not trying to boil the ocean, and might be followed by the recommendation that one tries to pick the 'low-hanging fruit' instead.

Bottom line

Put simply, the bottom line is the profit you make after everything has been taken into account. Politicians adore the phrase, and preface many of their remarks with 'the bottom line is ...'

Bring to the table

Easy to visualise but so, *so* 1990s that the phrase should be banished to the wilderness immediately. Just what does 'bring to the table' bring to the table? The answer is a shriek of disgust from anyone who is fond of the English language.

Buy-in

You are going nowhere if you do not have this in business. It means people agreeing with your idea or proposal.

Camel's nose is under the tent, the

A colourful and not too objectionable way of saying that a precedent is about to be set.

Can-do attitude

Nearly every recruitment ad that appears in our newspapers and on the Internet insists that the applicant have this particular quality. There is no record of any job-seeker claiming to possess a 'can't-do attitude' in his or her curriculum vitae.

Cash cow

This is probably a bit of an affront to the dairy herds of Ireland but businesses that produce a constant stream of revenue for their owners and shareholders tend to be likened to the humble cow with her milk-producing habits.

Cash injection

Businesses no longer receive extra money – they receive a cash injection, which sounds a bit more painful but is usually administered with a clean needle.

Centres of excellence

We may have low opinions about certain companies, but not even we would expect them to brand new or existing facilities as 'centres of mediocrity'. It is quite insulting to those mere mortals who value their contribution but find themselves operating outside such 'centres'. The use of the expression 'centres of excellence' should be confined to international rugby stars.

Challenging
This is one of the words that has lost all its meaning when used in business. It is the word that hides a multitude of facts. A company that has just had a horrendous year and has seen its profit margins squeezed to bits will often admit to having had a 'challenging' twelve months. Equally, the business that faces a future of uncertainty because it is not selling its products in sufficient quantities will speak of 'challenges ahead'. Just do not believe them.

Channel
Once upon a time, there was the English Channel and TV channels. Today, there are so many channels that one wonders if the earth's future is at stake. Admittedly, the word 'area' never sounded great either and was overused and misused. But 'channel' is definitely one for the ambitious types whom the Celtic Tiger economy has spawned. So here's a bit of advice. The Irish entrepreneur who isn't developing in a number of channels, preferably simultaneously, should be ignored or starved of that venture capital funding you were thinking of throwing his or her way.

Circle back around
This means putting off consideration of something until another time. Occasionally, that 'other time' equals 'never'.

Clear blue water
This is what you put between you and the competition when

those profit margins increase. Stylish-sounding, but would it not be simpler to say 'we have moved ahead of our rivals'?

Client-specific
This comes from the same hyphen-word family as customer-focused, only it is worse. The company is offering you a 'solution' that is specifically 'tailored' to your needs. In all probability, if it was not suitable for you, you would not have looked for it in the first place.

Closure, to bring
In the old days, there were simple verbs like 'to close', 'to finish off' and 'to round off' but none could quite compare with the most common of practices today, 'to bring closure'. It usually applies to an unsavoury or utterly forgettable episode.

Comfort zone
The place where no company can afford to be as global competition intensifies and survival in this high-cost economy of ours becomes ever more difficult. It has suffered through overuse.

Connectivity
This noun started life in the computer industry but moved into the mainstream of the modern English language without much resistance. A group protesting Aer Lingus's decision to withdraw its daily service from Shannon to Heathrow in 2006 called itself the Atlantic Connectivity Alliance. Is it any wonder its campaign failed?

Continuous improvement
This has almost become a science; how companies continually

improve what they do. It is now a specialist skill, even though it seems a fairly straightforward concept for any enlightened company to seek to do what they do a little better.

Co-opetition

One of those horrendous combination words that brings together the simple concepts of competition and co-operation, tries to make them into something altogether more profound and fails miserably to do so.

Core competencies

These are appearing in a mission statement near you on a regular basis. They are the things you are good at, stupid. No, they are the things you are very good at. What would corporate life be without core competencies? Business people with no concern for the sanctity of the English language use this expression with abandon.

Correction

The Central Bank of Ireland is renowned for its caution, so when its research suggested that the housing boom was about to end, it steered clear of using the 'f' word – falling, as in prices. Instead, it reached for the word 'correction', which is its way of saying that the market value of houses for the last decade was a 'mistake'.

Cross-functional

Just one of many terms used to describe the need for versatility and flexibility in the workplace. It is widely used in job recruitment ads to intimidate the hell out of applicants.

Crunch

The verb and noun are perfectly decent paid-up members of the English language, but when the adjective is introduced, for example, 'crunch talks', one wearies a bit. Is 'crunch' more urgent than 'crucial' or 'decisive', for instance?

CSR

Corporate Social Responsibility is the new name for voluntary or charitable acts that companies carry out. Many companies seek public recognition for their CSR efforts, and, thus, it is hard to escape the feeling that they see them as a way of enhancing their image among existing and potential customers. In the old days, companies went about their acts of generosity with a little less fanfare.

Customer-centric

This phrase is found frequently in recruitment ads. The notion that, in order to be successful in business, it is important to look after the customer, is not one that has just emerged after decades of scientific research. Perhaps those who use the term think it is a notch above 'customer-focused'. It is not.

Customer-focused

Name me a company that is not customer-focused and I will name you an entry in the list of failed enterprises. The problem is that companies nowadays boast that one of their attributes, usually a 'key' one, is this self-same focus on customers. We should all be grateful, I suppose, that they are even thinking of us.

Cutting-edge

This term is up there with 'leading edge' as an utterly useless and unnecessary adjectival phrase. Companies tend to proclaim that they are 'at the cutting edge'. Unless they are makers of scissors or saws, they should desist.

Damning indictment

This worn-out phrase is dusted down and trotted out any time a well-paid expert presents a report that casts a none-too-positive light on some part of Irish business. For example, foreign exchange over-charging at Allied Irish Banks (AIB) in 2004 was a 'damning indictment' of our regulatory controls in the financial services sector. Nobody dared disagree.

De-hire

It cannot be too long now before a company is set up to provide businesses around the world with a pleasant way of telling their staff that the jobs they once had no longer exist. Or am I ignoring the existence of public relations companies? Not quite as bad as a 'separation agreement' but de-hire has to be one of the more callous additions to the lexicon.

Deliver

There was a time when letters and parcels had this verb to themselves, but today it is not unknown for individuals or companies to deliver opportunities, savings, results, change and improvements, often all together and at once, with no concern for meaning whatsoever.

Dial-in

This means to include something. For example, 'we need to dial-in the increased price of raw materials'.

Dial-up

This is becoming a popular verb with marketing types. In times past, dialling up would have been what you would have done on that clunky telephone in the hallway. Today, it is used as a substitute for 'crank up' or 'ratchet up'. Why? Don't ask me.

Drive

This is another blight on the business landscape. It is the case that you no longer develop a business, but drive it, forward most of the time. Other things you are likely to drive are profits, productivity and turnover. 'Driving organisational change' is also a popular pursuit.

Drivers

There is the verb 'drive' and we now introduce you to the noun. Nothing to do with taxis or trucks, but everything to do with the way the English language has been amended to explain what happens in business. The noun is often preceded by the popular adjective 'key', as in 'key drivers of our business performance this year were the record number of housing starts and the many projects taking place under the National Development Plan'.

Down-climb

This noun was introduced into public discourse early in 2008 by US Secretary for Finance, Henry 'Hank' Paulsen, who just could not bring himself to admit that the domestic economy was in recession, so invented this noun instead.

Downscale

This is part of the family of words used liberally to describe how a company reduces its workforce without actually saying it in as many words. Like 'downsize', it is becoming too dark a word for many companies.

Downside

This means the 'bad news' dressed up, and is in such common use in business that rarely does a stockbroker's report appear without at least a dozen mentions of it.

Downsize

This verb has been practically abandoned by business in the 21st century, probably because it comes too close to expressing a negative concept like making a company smaller.

Downtime

It is no longer sufficient to have 'time off' or breaks from work. The new mantra is 'downtime', and how we do not get enough of it. Originally, the term applied to machines and equipment.

Drill down

There was a time not so long ago when we would begin consideration of a proposal at a meeting and then choose to 'go into more detail on it' at a later stage. But the oil industry exerts such influence in the world today that this practice has now become known as 'drilling down'.

Ducks in a row

If you have not got those ducks the way the man says, it means that you are not properly set up or prepared. It is was one in a spellbinding array of metaphors used by former Irish rugby coach Eddie O'Sullivan who at one stage also suggested that his team of grown men needed to take 'baby steps'.

Earnings dilutive

This phrase occasionally appears in stockbrokers' reports. It means that some part of your business is not as profitable as before, but is a way of saying it that almost makes it sound like an achievement.

Eighty/twenty rule

This term is straight out of the business handbooks and is becoming a more and more frequently used expression in Irish business. It is the statistic that says that most companies tend to do 80 per cent of their business with 20 per cent of their customers. It is probably true, but let us just say that and forget the shorthand version – please!

Elephant in the room

One of the most popular expressions in public debate, it originated in the United States and is used to describe a big problem that everyone is ignoring because it is socially or politically embarrassing. It can often be misused, with some speakers coming up with combinations such as the 'gorilla in the room' or the 'elephant in the kitchen'.

Elevator pitch

You have 60 seconds to sell your business idea to a potential investor. Hence, the name 'the elevator pitch', presuming that the building you are in hasn't just three floors.

Embrace

It is no longer good enough to make changes or merely to change. Politicians, trade unionists and chief executives will tell you that you must 'embrace' it.

Empower
The verb 'to empower' is one that has become frequently used in this era of partnership between employers and staff. Bosses who have just recently read the latest book on management techniques may well come into the office on a Monday morning and declare their intention to 'empower' staff. The word may trigger bewildered looks all round.

Evoision
The Revenue Commissioners and tax advisers continually make a distinction between 'tax evasion' and 'tax avoidance'. The former is against the law, the latter is legal, and the word above has come into being to explain the grey bit in between.

Facetime
This has come straight across the Atlantic from the United States and is another way of describing a meeting with your boss or colleague. Usually, workers complain they do not get enough of it with the people who matter.

First-mover advantage
The law of business that says if you get there first, you will most likely succeed over your competitors.

Flexicurity
This is a dastardly word that has become popular in the European Union to explain the importance of creating jobs that offer both 'security' and 'flexibility'. Apparently, it began life in Denmark.

Flexponsive
Just when you think it cannot get much worse, along comes another

double combination word to make you weep. IBM Global Services was responsible, we believe, and is trying to convey the idea of a company being both 'flexible' and 'responsive'.

Flogging

This is using a blog to 'astro-turf'. In others words, writing a glorious review of a hotel that you just also happen to own. See *astro-turf*.

Front of mind

This is the 21st-century way of telling someone you have not forgotten about them, that their particular needs and demands are 'front of mind'. In the past, being high up on the 'list of things to do' was the lengthier but saner way of saying it.

Fundamentals

As debate continues about what lies in store for the Irish economy, the optimists are able to summon up the 'fundamentals' and declare with great certainty that they are 'sound'. It has now become the catch-cry of government ministers who have finally woken up to the fact that those days of bumper State revenues were never going to last forever. One witty economist has given these politicians a nickname – the 'fundamentalists'.

Future-proof

This is one ugly hyphenated word that is commonly used by sellers of all sorts of products and services to convince potential buyers that they must make this purchase to secure their future. Given the uncertainty of what lies ahead, I am not sure that 'future-proofing' is even remotely possible to do.

Geographies

You think you have heard of every heinous crime committed against the English language and then along comes 'across the geographies'. Check any dictionary and you will see no mention of 'geographies'. The term is now widely used by companies with operations in different countries to explain how their businesses are doing in those countries. Unfortunately, 'across the geographies' has replaced 'in different countries'. We recommend that it be run aground somewhere.

Going forward

One of the great nothing expressions of our time. We are not sure where 'going forward' came from or where it is going to, but rumour has it that it was nowhere to be seen five years ago. It needs to make itself scarce.

Granularity

Some chief executives have taken to the word granularity like the proverbial 'ducks to water'. They will happily tell analysts and journalists that it will be a while before the company has more detail or 'granularity' on a particular subject such as profits.

Grey hair

When inexperienced entrepreneurs set up a business, they are often advised to take on some 'grey hair', i.e. to put it at its kindest, people of mature age who have loads of business expertise and experience they can give to the young 'whippersnappers'.

Grow the business

We know what it means, but does that make it less offensive?

'Our business is growing' is perfectly acceptable and the distortion of it deserves to be dispensed with immediately. Grammatically, it is a case of too many intransitive verbs being used transitively, 'progress' being another fine example.

Headcount

A concerted effort has been made over the last decade or so to take any human dimension out of places of work. So, when jobs are lost, it is now common for companies to announce a 'reduction in headcount', a pretty nasty way of describing the process by which employees who may have given long and loyal service to a company lose their jobs. One recruitment company in Ireland has seen the potential of the word and has called itself 'Headcount Solutions'.

Heads up

This is an expression beloved of the men and women of the public relations industry. Rarely a day passes without some PR person offering us a 'heads up'. Put simply, they are giving us notice of a forthcoming event that they wish us to cover. Up to now, the journalists of Ireland have shown great patience and have stopped short of boycotting regular users of the expression. But our patience stretches only so far. We want a return to the old-fashioned: 'We are ringing you about a forthcoming event.'

Helicopter view

This is the term for those who stand and look at their business from a distance or, in this instance, from a height.

Heritage

This word has been hijacked by companies barely in business a wet week but which are mad keen to tell potential customers that their proud ancestors date back to the Middle Ages at the very least.

Hero to zero
This is fast gaining popularity and is used to explain the plight of some high-profile figure or other being found to have feet of clay after all. The media usually create them in the first place, and relish their fall from grace.

Hit the ground running
What is so wrong with just saying 'get off to a fast start'?

HPSU
This is the sort of company you want to be in. The acronym stands for High Potential Start-Up and it is a phrase beloved of the state agency Enterprise Ireland. As the words suggest, it describes new companies that have a bright future.

Human resources
Once upon a time, there were people known as heads of personnel departments. They were in charge of the people working in a company who were responsible for recruitment. But that title was deemed to be inadequate and so Directors of Human Resources were born. They have not looked back since.

Impaired lending
A really sweet way of describing bad loans or debts, but do not be fooled. They are still bad loans.

Innovation
If there were an International Court for the Humane Treatment

of Nouns, innovation would have a very strong case, as would its first cousin, the verb 'to innovate'. It is uttered with abandon by people who want to send the message that, far from being stale and tired, they are 'innovating' at a frightening rate.

Internationalise

If there were a beauty contest for new verbs that have found their way into the English language in recent years, this would not be allowed to get into a swimsuit. It is most often used to describe companies that would like to start selling their products and services overseas.

Jaws

An expression used by bankers to describe the gap between income and costs. It would be preferable if they stuck to the simpler version.

Joined-up thinking

The trendy way of describing how different parts of a company, or a department of state, should work together to ensure that everyone is pursuing the same goals. Its origins must be a throwback to Junior Infants when we learnt about 'joined-up writing'.

Key

The Irish economy would grind to a halt if it were not for 'key'. Key is omnipresent: key deliverables; key solutions; key interventions; key drivers; Key Performance Indicators; key roles. Indeed, there is a danger that every business activity will soon be prefaced with this word.

Key influencers

You know you have arrived when you are described as one of these. If the public knew about some of the people that have been given this accolade, they might emigrate.

Keynote

This is a first cousin of 'key' and is often used to describe the most important address at a business conference. The only problem is how to work out what is the most important contribution of the day when each of them is described as a 'keynote address'. A more keynote address than others perhaps?

Key takeaway

This sounds like the way you might describe the Chinese food delivered to your doorstep after you have had a long, hard day at the office. This is an expression beloved of stockbrokers, who tend to interchange it with 'downside'. 'An important feature' sounds much nicer.

Kicking the tyres

One of those imports from the United States which, thankfully, is not as widely used in 2008 as it was a few years ago. It means testing something, and is to be avoided.

Knowledge economy

There are taxi drivers in Dublin who can hold informed conversations with you about the 'knowledge economy'. It is even reported that intimate contact between individuals has decreased dramatically because everyone is too busy embracing the knowledge economy. There are no known side-effects, but we are told that if we abstain, we could be in trouble. All those jobs in old-fashioned, low-skilled manufacturing are destined for China, India and Eastern Europe, and Ireland's future lies in investing in the life sciences, such as biotechnology, and in general research and development. So, because this places a greater emphasis on what is in our heads rather than what we can do with our hands, we are told that the trick is for Ireland to become a 'knowledge economy'. Some day we shall wake up and there will be a government announcement that we have become one.

KPI

Key Performance Indicators are annual statistics other than financial results which indicate how well a company is performing. The acronym is popular in the mobile phone business. As the country that gives companies like O_2 and Vodafone some of their highest profits per customer, Ireland tends to produce some very positive KPIs.

Leading-edge technology

Doubtless the technology would not have been developed in the first place were it not for the fact that it had some 'edge' to it. The boast that it actually is 'leading edge' is overdoing it.

Learning curve

This is a very convenient little expression to excuse all sorts of under-performance. It can be used to explain a multitude of situations. It conveys humility – 'I think we are all on a learning curve' is an expression often uttered by a politician when his policy to introduce new taxes turns out to be a proposal that could pretty swiftly bring about the collapse of the government of which he is a member.

Learnings

Where did this come from? We are not quite sure but it is often prefaced by the adjective we make reference to elsewhere – 'key'. It is another word for 'lessons' but has neither grace nor style.

Legacy

IT companies in business a wet week will talk about their 'legacy' as if they had been with us since time began. Interspersed with heritage.

Level playing field

The most elusive bit of real estate in Irish business and also common in other spheres of Irish society. The underdog telecoms provider who is tired of eircom's domineering presence will complain bitterly and regularly about the absence of one. If you had a euro for every time a business person declares 'All we are looking for is a level playing field', you would be wealthy beyond your wildest dreams.

Lifecycle

It used to be sufficient to describe that journey from birth to death as one's life but that has clearly proved inadequate for some, including the authors of the new Irish partnership deal, Towards 2016.

Low-hanging fruit

This is the easy business a company goes after. Geddit?

Mainstream

At first sight, there may be questions about its inclusion in this lexicon of jargon and clichés, but I talk not of the perfectly innocent noun but of its use as a verb. 'To mainstream' something has become a preoccupation of many companies. It is truly sad.

Major

An adjective that is much abused in public discussion today. Most often spotted in front of 'breakthrough', 'initiative' and 'programme', and very rarely merited.

Matrix

Slowly but surely, this noun is making its way into common use. One financial services company sought from potential job applicants 'an ability to communicate in a matrix environment', a sure sign that it's here to stay. The easiest definition of matrix we could find is 'an arrangement of connected things'. Now, if we can only work out how to communicate in it . . .

MBW

An acronym for Management By Walking, not too common in Ireland, but an American import that describes the chief executive officer who runs his business not behind a desk by remote control, but out walking through the plant, talking to staff and customers.

Meaningful

One perceptive journalist recently described it as one of the most 'meaningless' words in the English language. He has a point. Just how many sets of 'meaningful discussions' have you been exposed to in your lifetime?

Migrate

This word used to apply to people who chose to move from one place to another in search of work or a better livelihood. Now, companies migrate on a regular basis, generally to new 'platforms'.

Milestone

Often preceded by the aforementioned adjective 'major' for effect, this word is used so often to describe unremarkable events that it has lost its impact. A similar fate has befallen 'watershed'.

Mindset

The way you view something at a particular moment in time, and the way others might tell you how important it is to 'change' it.

Mission-critical

This is probably straight out of NASA headquarters in Florida, but it has infiltrated the world of Irish business and is too often found in recruitment advertisements. 'Important' is a much better word to use.

Moving the goal posts

Wouldn't you know, just when you have grasped the concept that has eluded you for years, you discover that those slender bits of timber that you had set your sights on have been taken and shifted over to the back pitch.

Multi-annual envelopes

These are the creation of officials in the Department of Finance to describe the new funding arrangements for departments of state. Instead of getting an annual budget, some departments with long-term spending plans are now being given commitments of money over a number of years. The Department of Health is a good example. And where is the money put but in multi-annual envelopes? The term strangely disappeared from the Budget speech for the 2006 fiscal year, giving rise to strong rumours that those envelopes had been shredded, but we understand that the money remains intact.

Multi-channel capabilities
This concoction has nothing to recommend it. It is just an ugly way of saying that something has more than one use.

Next steps
This expression was used a lot by Fianna Fáil in the run-up to the 2007 General Election to explain what they intended to do if returned to office for a third consecutive term. Well, get returned they did, and presumably, they're taking those 'next steps'.

Noise
A noun that is used to explain any distractions or disruptions to a normally smooth flow. Often used by companies to explain the sudden appearance of lower profits; in other words, losses they didn't foresee.

Offering
Perhaps the world of business is undergoing some biblical transformation without our knowledge, but everything it produces nowadays seems to be dressed up as an 'offering'. It almost encourages us to feel grateful, until we see the price.

Offline

A term for the IT age, the new version of 'off the record', describing some matter that would be better discussed somewhere other than the forum you happen to be in at the time.

On-board

A strange new verb which tries to describe the process by which an employer succeeds in signing up his employees for a new idea at work. The employer seeks to 'on-board' his staff to something. Horrendous.

On my radar

The new way of telling someone that they are in your thoughts or plans. To be told you are 'not on the radar' is the ultimate insult and putdown.

Operationalise

This six-syllable monster is on a par with 'internationalise' and has no redeeming features.

Outcomes

The plural of the noun has taken the place of plain old 'results' in many companies, and it just does not sound right at all.

Out of the loop

This describes the status of the manager who has just seen his department undergo a significant change without his boss telling him about it. It usually precedes his departure.

Package

Senior executives used to be paid wages. Now they get packages, the term used to describe those added extras, such as fancy cars and pension payments. The word tends to be used by those who have moved from one job to another and are not too keen to reveal that their basic salaries have been reduced or have stayed the same.

Paradigm shift
This is an expression beloved of companies that want to change the way they do things but cannot bring themselves to describe it in simple terms. So, in order to survive, the company has to move from its current model, or paradigm. Hence the shift.

Partnership
The old-fashioned adversarial language that dominated industrial relations in the1970s and '80s has been replaced by the concept known as partnership. Employers will often say they are keen to work in partnership with workers to save costs so that they can both survive. That can often be code for: you have two choices – you either row in behind what we say, or you face redundancy.

Perfect storm
It used to be the preserve of the weatherman, but now economists will trot it out to explain how a combination of currency flows, interest rates and dubious loans is creating the sort of conditions that are not good for the global economy.

Platform
We talk not of trains, or those fashionable '70s shoes, but what companies in the IT sector and elsewhere jump from regularly. Many 'platforms' tend to be 'enhanced' or 'innovative', but the

'platforms' that most businesses want to be on are those 'with a global reach.'

Players

Our company bosses love sporting metaphors. They will talk about 'wins' as if they were heading for the top of the English Premier League. But, most of all, they love to be players. Preferably 'key' players, but any sporting association makes them feel good about themselves.

Pressing all the right buttons

It is no longer enough to be just 'doing all the right things'. In this era of rapidly changing information and communications technology, the expression is popular with management consultants.

Proactive

In the last decade, it has never been sufficient for any businessperson worth his or her salt to be active. 'Proactive' has been the minimum requirement. It means self-starting, or showing some initiative.

Punch above one's weight

This falls into the 'seriously overused' category and should perhaps be put back from where it comes – the boxing ring.

Pushback

Not too frequently used, but when you are encountering 'pushback', it means you are meeting resistance to that plan of yours to reduce your staff's wages by ten per cent.

Put this one to bed

It sounds, when first heard, like a curt instruction to a misbehaving child to make themselves scarce but is, in fact, an expression used by business people to convey their eagerness that a plan or a deal be completed as soon as possible

Putting down a marker

This is an exercise beloved of the trade union movement. It often arises in the period immediately before the start of talks on a new partnership deal with the government, employers or voluntary groups in society. The marker tends to be put down, and then picked up swiftly enough, once the trade unions smell a decent pay rise. It also became a favourite expression of the Irish rugby players in the run-up to the World Cup in 2007, but their disappointing performance suggested that they could not find the marker, let alone place it anywhere significant.

Quantum leap

When a leap in itself is not sufficient, the adjective 'quantum' can be attached for greater impact.

Race to the bottom

This term has become a popular way of describing what employers are up to when they choose to exploit workers by paying them less than the minimum wage. Irish Ferries epitomised the so-called race to the bottom in November 2005 when they sought to replace Irish workers with lower-paid Latvian employees. A nation rebelled, and the company ended up giving the Latvian workers the minimum wage.

Raising the bar

This simply means making things more difficult and is in the 'too-frequently-used' category.

Ramping up

One day, you have a modest, three-employee company. Then you win a big contract, and suddenly you are 'ramping up'. Its origins are in the IT industry. It should be replaced by much more simple concepts such as developing, getting bigger or expanding. There are plenty of ways of not saying 'ramping up'.

Re-

The prefix has taken up residence at the beginning of so many words that it could possibly have a case for persistent overuse – among the favourites are rebalance, repurpose, reposition, restructure, re-engineer and retask.

Reality checks

We all need them, don't we? Although perhaps the expression is not as commonly used as it once was. Horror of horrors, it has been replaced by the ubiquitous 'wake-up calls'. What is wrong with 'warnings'?

Rebalancing

This is an interesting one. It tends to be trotted out when a company is selling a loss-making business in order to halt the drain on its finances. It has a wide application and can also be used by companies that are laying off hundreds of employees but cannot bring themselves to say it in so many words.

Re-sized

I'll wager my life savings that there are no examples in business anywhere of the verb 're-sized' being used to describe a company that is expanding its operations. No, the term 're-size' is a soothing way for company bosses to say that the reason they are able to pay a bigger than normal dividend to their shareholders is that they have laid off tens of thousands of workers around the world.

Respectabilise

Just what did the simple combination 'make more respectable' do to deserve being cast off and replaced by this objectionable five-syllable verb?

Revenue-generating unit

A close inspection of this term reveals that it is the way your average accountant or financial controller describes customers.

Rightsize

Becoming more popular among companies that do not want the word 'downsize' featuring in a press statement announcing that they are reducing the number of their employees. This is one of those cunning little words that aims to deceive, but most normal people have no difficulty seeing right through it.

Road map

This word started out life in the world of politics (think George W. Bush and the Middle East) but it has now gatecrashed the world of business. Companies that are running into difficulties tend to talk about having a 'road map' to get themselves out of trouble. A 'plan' is much simpler.

Robust

The dictionary definition is 'strong, healthy and durable', but more often than not, today a company boss uses it to describe the performance of his business, even though it has barely managed to keep going amid rising costs and reduced profits. Politicians, too, are becoming fond of the word, offering 'robust' responses to difficulties that arise in the health service or criminal justice system.

Rocket science

Usually preceded by the words 'it is not' and used widely to explain to people, who have a habit of looking blankly at their superiors when they are told to do something, that the task they are being set could be, well, performed by someone of tender years, say a three-year-old, for instance?

Rolling out

This used to apply to the red carpet. Nowadays it can apply to any new product or service that a company intends to launch on an unsuspecting public. Its use is a minor crime compared to some of the violence inflicted on the English language, but what is wrong with 'introducing'?

Safety-critical

During 2008, a spokesman for Iarnród Éireann explained its refusal to employ someone with diabetes on the basis that the job itself was 'safety-critical'. I think he meant that the job carried heavy safety responsibilities.

Scaleable

The ability of a company to grow gradually to meet the demands of new business opportunities.

Scope
Often used today as a verb. For instance, busy entrepreneurs will 'scope some time' for an afternoon meeting with a client. And just what was wrong with 'finding some time'?

Sea change
In the beginning, there was dramatic change and fundamental change. Out of nowhere, and at no one's invitation, along came 'sea change'. It is the catchphrase of companies that wish to let us know they have, er, changed. Why not plain 'change'?

Share of wallet
A term used by bank salespeople to describe their aim of extracting as much money from the customer as possible. Obviously, their bonus payments are dependent on securing a bigger share of what's in your wallet.

Shooting the breeze
You are standing in the corner of the office discussing your reservations about the chief executive's management style when along comes the said person and asks you what you are doing. 'Shooting the breeze', you lie.

Silver bullet
This expression is usually preceded by the words 'there is no ...'. It is another way of saying there is no instant, immediate solution to a particular problem.

Singing from the same hymn sheet
Does everyone know what the expression means? If not, discard it, because there are easier ways of saying that you are doing or saying the same thing or are 'at one'.

Skill set

There was a time when that recruitment advertisement suggested that you should have skills to qualify for a certain position. Nowadays you require a whole set of them. It conjures up an image of a little box you have under your bed at home which you take out every time you get called for an interview. Then you bring it in and lay it on the table in front of you. 'Here's me skill set' you tell the puzzled interviewers, with a nonchalance suggesting that it was your Lego set you had brought in with you.

Socialise

At last, you say, you recognise a word and presume that it's the verb used to describe when you go out for dinner with friends, head down to the local pub for a pint and a glass of wine. But in some businesses, 'socialise' has come to mean asking people about a certain idea or project so as to establish if it could have 'traction' or not.

Soft

In today's business world, a host of words is used to describe a product or service that is not performing to expectations. A spokesman disappointed with his company's performance will tell us that the USA was a 'soft market' for them. It usually means that the product hardly sold, but you can't say that, can you?

Soft landing

The housing market in Ireland defied every economist's prediction and forecast for over a decade. Then, almost without notice, prices dropped dramatically, but there were not thousands of people left on the roadside. This allowed most commentators to claim we indeed achieved a 'soft landing', rather than a cataclysmic bang and bust.

Soft launch
The term used to describe official openings and announcements where the client has not seen fit to invite a big name to do the needful. Often it is code for 'we do not expect much publicity, so why waste money on it?'

Solutions providers
In the pre-computer age, the world of work was composed of plumbers, teachers, nurses, doctors, builders, lawyers, journalists, bankers and a host of other recognisable trades and professions. But cometh IT, cometh the solutions providers. Go online and check how many solutions providers there are in the world. You never knew the planet had so many problems, did you? If you have a problem, there are millions of solutions providers just waiting to pounce and relieve you of your hard-earned money. And how can you spot one for sure? Their website will tell you that they are 'solution-driven'.

Smell test, a
An unpleasant sounding exercise that is used in business to describe the process that used to be called checking something out.

Space
There was a time when people worked in a sector or specialism. Today, they work in a 'space'. Business people of all backgrounds use the word so regularly that there is a real danger of clutter and congestion.

Stakeholder

This word became popular when Tony Blair was first elected British Prime Minister in 1997, and was an attempt by so-called New Labour to make voters feel loved and cared for. It has infiltrated the language of business and politics in Ireland too and is often used by public company bosses as a catch-all phrase for customers, shareholders and staff.

State-of-the-art

I doubt if it serves any purpose to be telling people that the fine extension you are adding to your existing plant is 'state-of-the-art'. Given the €5 million you are spending on it, and the likelihood that your business is biotechnology, most people would presume that it is not a tumbledown shack bolstered by second-hand materials and vulnerable to 70-mile-an-hour winds. 'State-of-the-art' is a worn-out cliché that deserves to be abandoned.

Staycations

Just to prove that jargon is being generated much more quickly than it can be suppressed, staycations was a term introduced by an advertising agency in the United States in 2007 to describe worried holiday-makers who, because of an economic downturn, were choosing not to vacation abroad but, yes, you've guessed it, 'staying' close to home, or at home.

Step change

This comes from the same family as 'sea change'. It is hard to work out whether or not it is a bigger change than 'sea change', but it does not stop company bosses from mentioning it to the media when they want to relay a message that they are not standing still.

Step up to the plate
Does anybody not know what this means? It comes from the game of baseball and means rising to the challenge. It is time to limit it to sport where it began its life.

Stickability
Advertising agencies use the word to measure the amount of time spent by Internet users on a particular website. Websites that hold users for more than a cursory glance are said to have good 'stickability'.

Stick to the knitting
An IT term used to describe companies that develop a product or service but do not spend their time enhancing its features or coming up with a new version.

Strategic
This adjective is much abused. It is often invoked to explain why a company is deciding to halve its workforce. Then there are those politicians who stop short of serious action on a proposal because they believe it important to take a 'strategic view'. Originally, it was used to distinguish vital longer-term thinking from day-to-day tactics.

Strategic thinking
It would be refreshing to come across a company in Ireland that is not thinking strategically. Most businesses have a simple strategy – making money – but others believe that unless they are thinking strategically from the time they rise in the morning until they put their head on the pillow at night, they are somehow deficient. We like deficient. The world of business would be a

better place if it was less strategic. After all, isn't it just a posh way of saying 'we have a plan'?

Stretch goal

Our first sighting of this barbarism was in the autumn of 2005. A goal is generally recognised as something you set your sights on, an objective. Tag on 'stretch' and it suggests something a little more, don't you think? And consultants got paid money for throwing in these limp adjectives?

Sub-optimal

What can you say about this one only that it ranges in meaning from 'not great', to 'pretty bad', to 'very bleak', and normally relates to the performance of the whole or part of a business.

Suite

When I was growing up, a suite was a big hotel bedroom for VIPs or what my brothers and sisters used to sit on in the sitting room. Now, it could be anything from a 'suite of products' to a 'suite of IT solutions'.

Sustainability

A new industry has been created out of the pursuit of sustainable business practices. 'Sustainability' is another word for not wrecking the planet as you go about making your big profits. It has become very fashionable.

Systemic

The culture of blame in Irish politics and public service is not that strong, so when serious mistakes are made, more often than not the investigations that take place usually end up pinpointing a 'systemic' rather than a 'personal' fault. You cannot sack a system, now, can you?

Tailored

It used to apply to suits, but today anything goes, although you will mostly find it placed in front of 'IT solutions'.

Take-outs

For a long while, we thought take-outs were to the United States what take-aways were to Ireland and Britain. Now, we discover that some business people have started using the word to describe what information or intelligence members of staff might take from a meeting or a training day. Quite often they are 'key take-outs'.

Tasked

This is the noun turned into a verb and used generally when senior executives find themselves in tight corners and have to explain what action is being taken; for example: 'I have tasked our head of human resources to ascertain if there was indeed a breach of protocol'.

Telcon

This abbreviated form of 'telephone conversation' is most likely to be found in emails, such as 'As per our telcon earlier, I now attach ...'

Temperature check

Medicine and meteorology meet business. Enough said.

The reality is ....

The beginning of many a statement made by business people and politicians, the phrase is always gratuitous. Just imagine beginning with the negative form – 'The reality isn't.'

Thinking outside the box

This phrase originated in the United States in the 1970s and related to a game similar to 'noughts and crosses' that had senior managers trying to come up with new ways of doing things. The exercise involved linking lines between boxes. We have paid a heavy price since for someone's creativity.

Thought-leader

A new species in the world of business who presumably think a little bit more than the average person. The whole idea of being a leader of thought smacks me as being, well, downright difficult in the first place. Just think about it – how can you lead someone's thoughts?

Ticking all the boxes

This is doing all the things you should be doing in your business. It is time to throw away the pen and tear up the bit of paper with the boxes on it.

Tight-hole confidentiality

This was contained in a press statement from an oil exploration company to explain that there was some top-secret drilling going on somewhere, and they could tell us nothing about it.

Tight-lipped

The clichés of journalism stubbornly refuse to disappear from print and the airwaves. In 2008, is it too much to expect that we might replace 'tight-lipped' with the much fresher and simpler 'saying nothing'?

Timebomb

It used to be just an explosive device which detonated after a certain period of time had elapsed. Now the word is most likely to be used to describe the worrying fact that about half the Irish population does not have a proper pension. To emphasise the point, it is best to add 'ticking'.

Time-poor

In the same category as 'downtime', another way of saying that I am working 14 hours, then have to pick up the kids from the crèche, go home and make the dinner and clean the house before going to the local residents' association meeting. Does 'time-poor' convey the anguish? I don't think so.

Time-rich

This describes that state of being for the lucky ones with time on their hands.

Tipping point

In the good old days, there were 'turning points'. Today, there are 'tipping points' and so many of them that we are not really sure whether or not they mean anything any more.

Tissue meeting

Gatherings that are popular in the marketing and advertising business and amount to preliminary discussions before serious discussions are entered into at subsequent meetings. 'Cloth' meetings perhaps?

Top of mind

Whether it is 'top of mind' or its first cousin 'front of mind', there are few uglier expressions in business today. It is another way of saying 'priority' or something that is high up on our list of things to do.

Toppy

A quaint little word that was much in evidence during 2005 at the time of some high-price property deals in Dublin. 'Toppy' means top-heavy or excessive and could be used to describe the price developer Seán Dunne paid for the four-acre Jurys Doyle site in Ballsbridge – a cool €250 million.

Touch base

Another baseball term that is frequently used by one business person who intends calling another businessperson later in the day to discuss some 'key deliverable'.

Traction

This has made its way from the physiotherapists' couch into the world of business. As the word suggests, it is used to describe something that has gripped or has been taken on or adopted by people. It is usually preceded by the verb 'gain'.

Transitions

One of those nouns that has been made into a verb by business people – a person 'transitions' to something else.

24/7

A novel concept for the first few years of its existence, but people now who tell you they are working 24/7 draw the sort of response previously reserved for those who came back from the United States after a two-week holiday with a distinctive 'I guess' twang.

Unique selling-point
Every salesperson worth his or her salt will wake up in the morning trying to work out that USP or unique selling-point.

Upside
This means the good news or the benefits and is regularly interwoven with the negative form, downside.

Up-skill
This is another horrendous hyphenated word that should be brought out to the backyard and shot. The best way of 'embracing' the 'knowledge economy' is to 'up-skill'. It is what people who are currently in low-skilled jobs must do if they are to hold on to their jobs, and secure higher-skilled jobs when their current ones disappear as a result of competition from China, India and Brazil.

Value chain
If you are not, as you read this, moving up the value chain, it may be too late. Put simply, it means that it is no longer enough for us to be making instant coffee. We have to be embracing Colombian. I know we are not coffee producers, but you get the gist. It is part of a process. We 'up-skill' the workforce, move up the value chain, and, in no time, we'll have our arms wrapped around the 'knowledge economy'. The worry is that with so many of us scrambling up that 'value chain', it could break under our weight and trigger a human catastrophe.

Value-drivers

Not low-fare taxis, but the newly discovered cost savings in a business that will mean cheaper products for customers.

VFM

No sooner is an expression coined, like 'value for money', than civil servants find an easier way of saying it. Eddie Hobbs became the consumers' champion in 2005 with his television series exposing the alleged rip-offs that lie at the heart of the Irish economy. Suddenly, it became a pretty good idea for our governing politicians to be banging the value-for-money drum. It was even more convenient when their civil servants shortened it to VFM.

Vigilance

This word beloved of central bankers means they are on the verge of increasing interest rates and making life more difficult for mortgage holders. Strong vigilance means that those rate hikes could be coming as soon as the next month.

Visibility

A noun that we used to associate with conditions for motoring, sailing and mountain climbing, among other pursuits, has now become a favourite of companies that want to tell their impatient analysts that things will become clearer at some unspecified time in the future.

Wake-up calls

There was a time when these calls were the preserve of mothers, keen to ensure that their sons and daughters got to school or work on time. Now, they are liberally sprinkled around the world of business and politics to describe some sudden event or other and its impact on behaviour. 'Wake-up calls' are to the twenty-first century what 'reality checks' were to the late twentieth.

Wash its face

Thankfully, this phrase is not in common use in Irish business – yet! It applies to a new business idea and whether or not it will pay for itself, at the very least.

Webinar

A seminar, except those taking part are linked over the Internet, via webcast. Appalling!

Window of opportunity

Double-glazed or single-glazed, it matters not a jot, that 'window of opportunity' opens and closes with more frequency than your average front door. Is it time we moved on and came up with a better metaphor?

Win-win situation

This phrase is not as distasteful as some other overused expressions, but it is in dire need of replacement. Most often used to describe the situation where both seller and buyer are seen to benefit, which is pretty fundamental to the pursuit of successful business, come to think of it. When a retailer sells a warm coat to a man who is cold and hasn't got one, and the price is reasonable, and both parties are happy, you've come across a 'win-win situation' at its simplest. There are plenty of other examples. Too many.

Working groups

These are beloved of politicians who, when presented with

reports urging some action on a matter, decide that it might not be the most popular move in the world and declare the need for the establishment of a working group to 'tease out some of the more complex' issues. The 'teasing out' tends to take quite a while, remarkably!

Work-life balance
A new library could be opened with the number of reports now published on how to achieve the perfect work-life balance. Some may have already reached this exalted state, but few ever get there.

Workplace
It used be the office, or the factory floor, or just plain work but now we have this noun that seems to cover every angle. Therefore, it is now violence in the workplace, stress in the workplace, and, most importantly, disenchantment in the workplace.

Year-on-year
As if this way of describing how a company compares its results from one year to another wasn't bad enough, along comes every stockbroker in town with the acronym, YOY. Why oh why? is right.